SO YOU THINK
YOU'RE A
BOSTON RED SOX
FAN?

SO YOU THINK YOU'RE A
BOSTON RED SOX
FAN?

STARS, STATS, RECORDS, AND MEMORIES FOR TRUE DIEHARDS

BILL NOWLIN

SPORTS
PUBLISHING

Sports Publishing books may be purchased in bulk at special discounts for sales promotion, corporate gifts, fund-raising, or educational purposes. Special editions can also be created to specifications. For details, contact the Special Sales Department, Sports Publishing, 307 West 36th Street, 11th Floor, New York, NY 10018 or sportspubbooks@skyhorsepublishing.com.

Sports Publishing® is a registered trademark of Skyhorse Publishing, Inc.®, a Delaware corporation.

Visit our website at www.sportspubbooks.com.

10 9 8 7 6 5 4 3 2 1

Library of Congress Cataloging-in-Publication Data is available on file.

Cover design by Tom Lau
Cover photo courtesy of AP Images

Interior photographs on the following pages are courtesy of Bill Nowlin: vii, 12, 26, 41, 54, 66, 91, 96, 98, 101, 104, 114, 121, 125, 126, 140, 154, 172

Interior photographs on the following pages are courtesy of the Boston Public Library: 20, 39, 63, 82, 85, 137, 149

Interior photograph on page 87 is courtesy of Johnny Pesky.

Print ISBN: 978-1-61321-974-4
Ebook ISBN: 978-1-61321-975-1

Printed in the United States of America

Contents

Introduction

So many things—and so many bizarre things—have happened in more than 116 years of Red Sox history that, in putting together a book like this, it's hard to know where to stop. The team clearly has a storied past. Even in very recent history, they've broken an 86-year-old "curse"—winning the final eight games of a most improbable 2004 postseason. And then they won two more world championships, the last one in 2013 following a pair of last-place finishes. There have been so many great players over the years, and so many characters, too.

Boston's Storrow Drive back in the dark ages, before "The Curse" was lifted.

If you're a real fan, you come to love a team—sometimes for better or worse, sometimes at the risk of one's own mental health. It can be like a family, weird uncles and all.

It was great fun writing this book, trying to think of some real stumpers and not just the easy questions. Some things that have happened in Red Sox history are pretty hard to believe, yet happen they did.

I hope everyone who reads this book will find something that truly surprises them. And I know there are plenty of other things out there . . . things no one's unearthed yet. There are things that are going to happen this coming year, too. Take note.

1

SPRING TRAINING

Through spring training 2016, the Boston Red Sox have played a total of 2,908 preseason exhibition games (they are 1,589–1,281, with 67 ties, the most recent tie being the 4–4 tie against the Pirates on March 30, 2016, in Bradenton).

Here's a question to kick off the book: Can you cite all the games the Red Sox won in spring training?

OK, we didn't really expect you to come up with that one. Now, let's get a little more serious.

1 First one real test: in 15 seconds or less, can you name the years in which the Red Sox won world championships? *(Answer on page 5.)*

2 What was the team name before it was the Boston Red Sox? *(Answer on page 5.)*

3 Can you name the first opponent the team ever played? This was in spring training, in April 1901. *(Answer on page 6.)*

4 Which of the following locales has never been the spring training home of the team? *(Answer on page 6.)*

Augusta, Georgia; Macon, Georgia; Little Rock, Arkansas; Hot Springs, Arkansas; Redondo Beach, California; Tampa; San Antonio; New Orleans; Bradenton; Pensacola; Savannah; Sarasota; Medford, Massachusetts; Baltimore; Pleasantville, New Jersey; Scottsdale, Arizona; Winter Haven, Florida; Fort Myers; Lee County, Florida.

5 Can you name the places outside the United States where the Red Sox have played preseason games? *(Answer on page 6.)*

6 While we're thinking of unusual locales or opponents, can you provide any of the details of the time (this was before Prohibition) when they Red Sox played a temperance society? *(Answer on page 8.)*

7 You will have noticed (if you read the answer to the previous question) that the Red Sox played some exhibition games in the middle of the season. What's up with that? It's just something teams used to do. They don't do it anymore. Omitting the situation in 2008, when was the last time the Red Sox played an in-season exhibition game? *(Answer on page 9.)*

8 When was the last time the Red Sox played an exhibition game after the season was over? *(Answer on page 9.)*

9 What is the largest crowd before which the Red Sox have ever played? *(Answer on page 10.)*

10 Did the Red Sox ever pitch a perfect game in spring training? *(Answer on page 10.)*

11 History repeating itself? What do Bobby Sprowl (1978) and Bryce Brentz (2013) have in common? *(Answer on page 11.)*

12 There was one year a star player for the Red Sox lasted less than one hour at spring training. Who was the player, what was the year, and why did his spring training last less than 60 minutes? *(Answer on page 11.)*

SPRING TRAINING ANSWERS

1 Those years are 1903, 1912, 1915, 1916, 1918, 2004, 2007, and 2013. So far. You got them all right? Say, maybe you *are* a Red Sox fan! But, really, don't feel bad if you missed a couple. Or had to look them up. You can still be a Red Sox fan. Immediate recall of facts and factoids doesn't really measure fanhood. You can still cheer for the Sox and root for them to win games, even if your head is not filled with all sorts of minutiae. Memorize every word of this book, though, and you can impress other Red Sox fans with your knowledge. Or else you can just have fun reading the book and marveling at some of the great accomplishments and odd moments throughout Red Sox history—even recent history, given that some of what's included here happened as recently as 2016.

2 From its inception in 1901 to December 18, 1907, the team was generally known as the Boston Americans. Some books like to call the earlier team by names such as the Boston Pilgrims, but before you do, see: Bill Nowlin, "The Boston Pilgrims Never Existed," in *The National Pastime*, #23, 2003, and a follow-up article

"About the Boston Pilgrims," *The National Pastime*, #26, 2006. For a good look at the very first year of the franchise, see the SABR book *New Century, New Team: The 1901 Boston Americans.*

3 The game took place on April 5, 1901. It was at Charlottesville, Virginia. The score was Boston 13, University of Virginia 0. Six days later, on April 11, the two teams played each other once more. This time, the score was 23–0 in favor of the professionals. Other than some intrasquad games, these were the only two preseason exhibition games played in 1901; thus, Boston concluded its first spring training with an aggregate score of 36–0.

4 In addition to Charlottesville, every one of the locales listed has at one time or another served as the team's spring training home, and in the order listed.

5 The team has played the following exhibition games outside the continental United States:

March 27, 1941 @ Havana, Cuba: Cuban Stars 2, Boston 1
3/28 @ Havana, Cuba: Boston 9, Cincinnati 2
3/29 @ Havana, Cuba: Cincinnati 6, Boston 3
3/30 @ Havana, Cuba: Cincinnati 2, Boston 1

March 9, 1946 @ Havana, Cuba: Washington 10, Boston 9
3/10 @ Havana, Cuba: Boston 7, Washington 3

March 26, 1965 @ Nogales, Mexico: Boston 15, Cleveland 9

March 25, 1966 @ San Juan Puerto Rico: Minnesota 9, Boston 0

3/26 @ San Juan, PR: Minnesota 3, Boston 1

3/27 @ Ponce, PR: Boston 5, Minnesota 1

March 31, 1967 @ Fredriksted, St. Croix, US Virgin Islands:
   New York Yankees 3, Boston 1

April 1, 1967 @ Charlotte Amalie, St. Thomas, VI: Boston 13,
   New York Yankees 4

March 20, 1978 @ San Juan, PR: Pittsburgh 5, Boston 4

3/21 @ Bayamon, PR: Boston 5, Pittsburgh 4

March 11, 2000 @ Santo Domingo, Dominican Republic:
   Houston 4, Boston 3

March 12, 2000 @ Santo Domingo, DR: Houston 3, Boston 2

March 22, 2008 @ Tokyo, Japan: Boston 6, Hanshin Tigers 5

3/23 @ Tokyo, Japan: Boston 9, Yomiuri Giants 2

April 1, 2016 @ Montreal, Quebec: Boston Red Sox 4, Toronto
   Blue Jays 2 (10 innings)

4/2 @ Montreal, QC: Boston Red Sox 7, Toronto Blue Jays 4

Note: One hundred years earlier, the Red Sox played their first game in Canada, an in-season exhibition game on July 24, 1916, at Toronto. The score was Boston 5, Toronto 5 (tie, 9 innings). In 1921, they played a game in London (Ontario) on

August 30 and lost: London Champs 5, Boston 3. Other Canadian exhibition games were August 26, 1930 @ Saint John, New Brunswick: Boston 7, Saint John 5.

1965

6/21 @ Toronto, Ontario: Toronto Maple Leafs (IL) 5, Boston 2

1966

6/20 @ Toronto, ON: Boston 8, International League All-Stars 4

1970

6/8 @ Montreal, QC: Montreal 8, Boston 6

1981

8/8 @ Montreal, QC: Montreal 5, Boston 4

6 If you can't, we can. It was on June 20, 1904, at Elmira, New York: despite the actual score being 5–4 Boston after nine innings and both teams scoring six runs after a full 11, the umpire ruled the game a 6–5 win for the Father Mathew Temperance Society. One wonders about the sobriety of the official scorer, who had mistakenly only counted three of Boston's four runs in the fourth and thus told manager Collins that the score was 5–4 Boston through eight. When the temperance society team scored once in the bottom of the ninth, both teams thought the score tied and so played until the FMTS team scored one more in the 11th. When the mistake was noted, the umpire ruled that since both teams willingly had played 11, the score should be deemed to have been tied before the "winning" run scored. The box score shows a 6–6 final, with the winning score being 6–5. This tidbit from the Bill Nowlin exhibition games database.

7 It was in 2005, on May 23, in what used to be an annual event at the National Baseball Hall of Fame in Cooperstown, New York. The Detroit Tigers beat the Boston Red Sox, 6–4. Since this was early in the season when the Red Sox were reigning World Champions for the first time since the 1918 World Series, the town was overrun with Red Sox fans. It was quite a spectacle. Pity the poor Tigers fan who turned up, though the final score may have given them a bit of solace. Major-league teams no longer grace Cooperstown for this event.

8 Yes, strange as it may seem, the team used to engage in some postseason exhibitions, before the days of broadcasting (when the revenues generated make organized baseball want to focus on the actual playoffs and World Series). In the first couple of decades, the team would sometimes play in the other five New England states and occasionally in other places. The last such game was on October 3, 1920, in Thompsonville, Connecticut: Boston 7, Bigelow-Hartford 1.

In 1946, while waiting for the National League pennant to be decided in a best-of-three playoff series against Brooklyn and in order to keep in playing shape, the Red Sox played three games at Fenway Park against a team of All-Stars, including Joe DiMaggio. In the October 1 game, Ted Williams was hit by a pitch on the elbow and left the game. There was some concern he wouldn't be able to appear in the World Series at all. He played, but was demonstrably subpar throughout. The Sox lost the middle game of the three tune-up games, 4–2.

9 It's in this section because it was a spring training game—even though it came after two games of the regular season had been played. The game took place on March 29, 2008, at Los Angeles. The final score was Boston 7, Los Angeles Dodgers 4, played before 115,300 paid at the Los Angeles Coliseum—the largest crowd to ever watch a baseball game, Red Sox or otherwise. Through a scheduling accommodation, the Sox had already played two regular-season games in Tokyo before coming back to the United States and tuning back up again while they got over jetlag. They played three games in LA, one of them the game at the Coliseum.

10 Yes, on March 14, 2000, at Fort Myers. The score was Boston 5, Toronto 0. The only perfect game thrown by the Red Sox in exhibition play was a combined effort of six Red Sox pitchers: Pedro Martinez, Fernando de la Cruz, Dan Smith, Rheal Cormier, Rich Garces, and Rod Beck. After it was over, Beck admitted, "I didn't find out about it until I turned around to shake the guys' hands and I looked up and saw it on the board. I saw 'perfect game' and I said, 'Hey, pretty cool.'" Cormier,

who'd pitched the seventh, was out in the parking lot talking to his wife when he heard about it. Smith and Garces both confessed they hadn't known it was a perfecto, either.

11 They both suffered preseason gunshot wounds. Lefthander Bobby Sprowl was shot in the right arm while he slept in his Winter Haven hotel room; the gun was fired by a doctor in the next-door apartment who said he thought he heard prowlers. Sometime in January 2013, Brentz managed to shoot himself in the leg while purportedly cleaning his handgun. The bullet went in one side and came out the other.

12 The player was Ted Williams. The year was 1954. Diving for a ball within an hour of suiting up for spring training, Ted Williams fell and broke his collarbone. He did not return until May 15. Though batting .345 at year's end, he only had 386 at-bats and lost the title to Bobby Avila (.341), since he was 14 at-bats short of the required 400. Ted walked a league-leading 136 times, however. A change was made, and later batting titles have been awarded based on plate appearances.

2

OPENING DAY

OK, the team's warmed up and hopefully worked out most of the kinks, and it's time to kick off the season.

You win some, you lose some. That's been true for Red Sox opening days. From 1901 through 2016, counting just the very first game, the team has won 58, lost 59, and had one tie. In three years, though, the team played doubleheaders on Opening Day. The team lost the second game of the 1903 doubleheader, likewise in 1948, and again in 1982. That makes the final total for Opening Day 58–62–1.

Let's start the questions.

1 Cy Young was the Opening Day pitcher six years in team history. There are two Red Sox pitchers who started even more Opening Day games. Can you name the two? *(Answer on page 17.)*

2 In all of Red Sox history, only three pitchers have won three consecutive Opening Days games. Can you name them? *(Answer on page 17.)*

3 It's one thing to start at your position several years in a row, and rarer than one might think. Imagine playing on

Opening Day five years in a row, but at a different position each year. There was a Red Sox player who once did that. Can you name him? *(Answer on page 17.)*

4 In the days of the 154-game schedule, teams typically opened the season in mid-April. Times have changed. What is the date of the earliest Opening Day in Red Sox history? *(Answer on page 17.)*

5 In 2016, Mookie Betts hit a home run on Opening Day, just as he had done in 2015. David Ortiz hit home runs on Opening Day 2016 and then hit another home run the very next day—and yet he was always known as a slow starter. Who was perhaps the most productive Opening Day batter in team history? *(Answer on page 18.)*

6 What was special about Dwight Evans's Opening Day home run in 1986? *(Answer on page 18.)*

7 Four Red Sox players have hit two homers in an Opening Day game. Can you name all four? *(Answer on page 18.)*

8 It really would be hard to argue against this choice for a home opener: who hit the most dramatic Opening Day home run in Red Sox history? *(Answer on page 19.)*

9 The Red Sox have hosted the Yankees 28 times for home openers, more than any other team. When was the last time the Red Sox lost a home opener to the New York Yankees? *(Answer on page 20.)*

10 In the 1969 season, something very unusual occurred in the first three games of the season. What was it? *(Answer on page 21.)*

OPENING DAY ANSWERS

1 The man with the most Opening Day starts is Roger Clemens with 10 (5–2, with three no-decisions). Pedro pitched seven openers (and was 3–1 with three no-decisions).

2 Two of them were known for their ability with the bat. The three pitchers are Babe Ruth (1916–18), Wes Ferrell (1935–37), and Pedro Martinez (1998–2000).

3 It was Jack Rothrock. In 1928, he was the Opening Day shortstop. In 1929, he played center field. He was the starting right fielder in 1930, the team's third baseman in 1931, and the left fielder in 1932. He played error-free ball all five openers. After the '32 season, he was traded away. While with the Red Sox, Rothrock played other positions during the regular season. On September 24, 1928, he pitched a hitless inning and on the 29th, he caught one inning just so he could say he had played all nine positions.

4 We could have added a huge hint. The game was the one played farthest from Fenway. It was March 25, 2008—at the Tokyo Dome in Japan. The Red Sox were reigning

world champions. Daisuke Matsuzaka was the starting pitcher. He was the first foreign-born player in American League history to start on Opening Day in his native land. (The first foreign-born pitcher to start a season for Boston was also the first pitcher to ever start for the team: Win Kellum of Waterford, Ontario, in 1901.) In the 2008 game, Brandon Moss homered in the top of the ninth to tie the game, 4–4. It was his first big-league homer. Manny Ramirez doubled in the top of the 10th, driving in two runs and making the difference in the ultimate 6–5 win over Oakland. Manny was named MVP of the game and given a large photocopy machine by sponsor Ricoh.

5 Try Ted Williams. It seems like he couldn't wait for the season to get started. "The Kid" batted in 15 Opening Day games, hitting .433 (23-for-53) with 42 total bases and 15 RBIs.

6 It wasn't just the first batter, but the first pitch. And it wasn't just the first pitch in the Red Sox game, but the first pitch in all of baseball. A great start to the season, but Evans was not that thrilled. He commented later, "No big deal. We lost."—*The Ultimate Red Sox Home Run Guide.*

7 This is a tough one. Ted Lepcio was the first to do it, on April 12, 1955. If you got that, that's very good. But then ten years later, to the day, Lenny Green hit two of Boston's five home runs in the April 12, 1965, opener. Yaz did it three years later, on April 10, 1968. And

Carlton Fisk did it on April 6, 1973—one of his homers a grand slam that helped pulverize the Yankees, 15–5. The 1973 game was the first major-league game to ever feature a designated hitter, but Red Sox DH Orlando Cepeda went 0-for-6. Fisk was, of course, the catcher.

8 Mo Vaughn. On April 10, 1998. Randy Johnson was the starter for Seattle. The Mariners led, 3–2, after seven innings, then scored two insurance runs in the top of the eighth and two more in the ninth. It was 7–2, Seattle, when the Sox came up to bat in the bottom of the ninth. We can understand that a lot of fans had left the park. Heathcliff Slocumb took over for the Big Unit. He faced three batters and didn't get anyone out. It was 7–3. Tony Fossas came on and walked the only man he faced. The third reliever of the inning was Mike Timlin. Nomar singled, and he hit John Valentin. He didn't get anyone out, either. Three pitchers had faced six Sox batters, three runs were in, and the bases were loaded with nobody out. The score was 7–5. Mariners manager Lou Piniella called for Paul Spoljaric to face Mo Vaughn. There wasn't any pitching around him, but Vaughn had already struck out three times in the game. Not this time. Grand slam! Game over! The Red Sox won, 9–7, in a walk-off.

The full story is told in the book *Love That Dirty Water: The Standells and the Improbable Red Sox Victory Anthem*, but a new Fenway Park tradition was born that day. Control room operator Kevin Friend was in charge of the sound system, and the music played at the ballpark. He chose that perfect moment to punch up the song on the park sound system. "It was an incredible, euphoric scene," he said. Now, within one second after every Red Sox home victory, "Dirty Water" is pumped throughout Fenway Park and jubilant fans proudly join in on the chorus—"Aw-oh Boston, you're my home!"

9 It's hard to believe it's been such a long time. The last time the Sox lost an Opening Day at home to the Yankees was in 1960. It was April 19, 1960, a 7–4 loss. Don Buddin was the shortstop and leadoff batter. Frank Malzone was on the team. So was Ted Williams, in his final year (he did drive in one of the Red Sox runs). Haywood Sullivan was the catcher. Tom Brewer was the starting pitcher. Since that time, more than half a century ago, the Sox have hosted the Yankees seven more times on Fenway's opening day and won every one of them.

Spring training photo at the Safari, Scottsdale, Arizona. L to R: Bill Monbouquette (with camera), Don Buddin, Rip Repulski, and Don Gile.

10 The first three games of the season were on April 8, 10, and 11, 1969—the Sox started the '69 season with three extra-inning games, each one longer than the one before. The first game was in Baltimore, a 5–4 win in 12 innings. A Dalton Jones sacrifice fly scored Tony Conigliaro (who was in his first major-league game after the horrific beaning he'd borne in August 1967). Tony had homered in the 10th to give Boston the lead, but Baltimore tied it back up. Two days later, in the season's second game, the Orioles won, in the 13th inning, with a double by Frank Robinson and a walk-off single by Boog Powell. The Sox traveled to Cleveland and played on the 11th. A low-scoring affair, it was 1–1 after nine. And still 1–1 after 14 innings. Rico Petrocelli singled, ran to third base on Russ Gibson's single, and then scored on a ground-out to second base by George Thomas. Bill Landis was the pitcher of record and got the win, already 2–0 on the season. Juan Pizarro had blown the first game in the 10th but earned a save in this one.

3

PATRIOTS DAY

Only two of the 50 states celebrate Patriots Day, so for most Americans it is often a holiday they only learn about later in life. The day—April 19—celebrates the first battle of the American Revolution, the battles of Lexington and Concord in Massachusetts in 1775. It is a state holiday in Massachusetts and Maine. (Why Maine? Maine used to be part of Massachusetts until it became its own state in 1820.) Every Patriots Day (since 1897), the Boston Marathon is held. And it is the one fixed date on the American League schedule: the Red Sox have to be home.

The first major-league baseball game played on Patriots Day in Boston was when the Boston Beaneaters played the game on April 19, 1895. (With the decision to celebrate most holidays on Mondays, Patriots Day is now deemed to be the third Monday in April.)

1 Speaking of the National League's Boston Beaneaters, can you name two of the 1895 Beaneaters team who later played for or managed the American League franchise now known as the Red Sox? *(Answer on page 25.)*

2 In 1902, when the two teams were actively warring, there were three games on Patriots Day—the Beaneaters played a doubleheader, and the Boston Americans played one game. In 1903, there were four big-league games in Boston: the Americans scheduled a 10:30 a.m. game as the first of two games (separate admission, with the Marathon finish in between them), and the Beaneaters played two, too. The progression was interesting. What happened in 1905? *(Answer on page 25.)*

3 When did it start that only the Red Sox held games on Patriots Day? *(Answer on page 25.)*

PATRIOTS DAY ANSWERS

1 How'd you do? There were only two: Jimmy Collins and Hugh Duffy. But if you were to look at the 1897 Beaneaters, the first year the Boston Marathon was run, you would have a significantly bigger pool: Collins, Duffy, Charlie Hickman, Fred Lake, Ted Lewis, and Chick Stahl.

2 The two teams worked out a schedule that saw them more or less alternate Patriots Day games, with the AL in town on the even-numbered years.

3 Unsurprisingly, it was when the Boston Braves left Boston in 1953 to move to Milwaukee. The last time the Red Sox were not at home on Patriots Day was in 1958. The morning game, now set for 11:05 a.m., is the only morning game on the major-league schedule.

Keeping score at Fenway

4

PITCHING

You can never get enough pitching. So the saying goes. Any Red Sox fan would agree. It's so frustrating to often have so many powerful hitters but see games slip away because of the lack of good, dependable pitching. This isn't the place for a rant on the subject: the Red Sox have had their great pitchers, too, ranging from Hall of Famer Cy Young (inducted 1937) to Hall of Famer Pedro Martinez (inducted 2015). Let's take some time and look a bit at pitching over the years.

1 Consider these 10 names. What name (if any) doesn't fit? *(Answer on page 39.)*
Roger Clemens
Cy Young
Tim Wakefield
Mel Parnell
Luis Tiant
Pedro Martinez
Joe Wood
Bob Stanley
Jon Lester
Joe Dobson

2 Cy Young threw 275 complete games for the Red Sox, a pretty astonishing feat in the present era of the six-inning "quality start." Which Red Sox pitcher ranks second on the list for number of complete games, and who was #3? *(Answer on page 40.)*
A. Pedro Martinez
B. Luis Tiant
C. Bill Dinneen
D. Roger Clemens
E. George Winter
F. Todd Anton

3 Who pitched in more games for the Red Sox than any other pitcher? *(Answer on page 40.)*

4 Who started more Sox games than any other pitcher? *(Answer on page 41.)*

5 Starting games is one thing, of course. Winning them is another. Which Red Sox pitcher (with 100 or more decisions) has the best career winning percentage during his time with Boston? *(Answer on page 42.)*

6 In the early days of baseball, there used to be pitchers who would take pride in being an "iron man"—for instance, pitching both games of a doubleheader. These days, like double features at a movie theater, the only doubleheaders you will find in baseball are separate admission doubleheaders occasioned by a postponed game being made up. And with the emphasis on pitch counts and the like, you won't find the same starter pitching both games.

Can you name the last Red Sox pitcher to start back-to-back games? *(Answer on page 42.)*

7 He's in the Hall of Fame, but he also holds the record for the most losses in a given season for the Boston Red Sox. In fact, he led the league in losses two years in a row. Who is he? *(Answer on page 43.)*

8 Which two Red Sox pitchers won the "Pitching Triple Crown"? *(Answer on page 43.)*

9 Which Red Sox pitcher threw a no-hitter in his Red Sox debut? *(Answer on page 44.)*
 A. Mel Parnell
 B. Billy Rohr
 C. Clay Buchholz
 D. Hideo Nomo
 E. Jon Lester

10 When did a Red Sox pitcher throw a nine-inning no-hitter despite giving up a clean base hit in the sixth inning? *(Answer on page 44.)*

11 True or false? Cy Young once pitched to more than 75 consecutive batters without giving up a hit. *(Answer on page 45.)*

12 A perfect game is, of course, one in which a pitcher retires 27 batters in a row without anyone reaching base by any means: walk, hit, error, hit-by-pitch, etc. Only Cy Young and Ernie Shore ever retired 27 consecutive batters in a single game. What Red Sox pitcher holds the record for consecutive batters retired, spanning more than one game? *(Answer on page 45.)*

13 To throw a no-hitter requires an exceptional pitching performance, but a catcher also has to be truly in sync with his pitcher. Can you name the four catchers who caught more than one no-hitter for the Red Sox? *(Answer on page 45.)*

14 This Red Sox pitcher worked a game in which he didn't give up a hit, either. He actually lost the game, one in which the other team's batters never even recorded an at-bat. How can you lose a game, without giving up a hit, and indeed without the opposition ever having an at-bat? This really did happen. Who was the pitcher and what was the story? *(Answer on page 47.)*

15 Besides Devern Hansack, there is another Red Sox pitcher who threw a complete game without yielding a base hit, but who is not included in the list of no-hit pitchers. Who is he? *(Answer on page 48.)*

16 This pitcher gave up a lot of hits of the four-base variety. He gave up homer after homer after homer and was left in to give up even more homers. Which Red Sox pitcher holds a record he no doubt would be glad to relinquish? *(Answer on page 49.)*

17 As recently as 2015, a Red Sox pitcher did something that had never been done in the American League for

100 years: he recorded at least 10 strikeouts in each of his first three starts with a team. You don't need a long memory for this one. Who was he? *(Answer on page 49.)*

18 How about this? You just start throwing strikes and don't stop. No one's ever thrown the most perfect of games, throwing 81 consecutive strikes—without a foul third strike. But one Red Sox pitcher opened a game by throwing nine strikes in a row and recording three outs, then taking his seat at the end of the first inning. We were told at the time that he was the only pitcher in American League history ever to have opened a game with three straight strikeouts on nine pitches. Who was the pitcher, and when was the game? *(Answer on page 50.)*

19 Which Red Sox pitcher holds the major-league record for averaging the highest number of strikeouts per nine innings pitched over the course of a season? *(Answer on page 51.)*

20 Which Boston Red Sox pitcher recorded the most strikeouts in one inning, thereby tying a major-league record? *(Answer on page 51.)*

21 How about walking almost everybody in sight? This Red Sox pitcher worked for four innings (thus recording 12 outs), but in the process he also walked 11 batters. Who was he? *(Answer on page 52.)*

22 You're a pitcher and you come in to pitch for the very first time in the major leagues. You might dream of mowing them down on nine strikes, but reality intrudes and you give up a home run. It's happened three times to Red Sox pitchers, when the first batter they ever faced in the big leagues hit a home run off them. Who were these three pitchers? *(Answer on page 53.)*

23 In these days when complete games are increasingly rare, it happens that two or more pitchers may sometimes combine to throw a shutout. The Boston Red Sox hold the major-league record for the most pitchers used in throwing a shutout. How many pitchers did they use? *(Answer on page 55.)*

24 Which Red Sox left-handed pitcher holds the American League record for the most shutouts thrown in one season? *(Answer on page 55.)*

25 Shutout after shutout. There were three Red Sox pitchers who each threw four consecutive shutouts—name them. *(Answer on page 56.)*

26 Which Red Sox pitcher has the most shutouts in the course of his Red Sox career? *(Answer on page 56.)*

27 Can you name four of the seven Red Sox pitchers who threw a shutout in their major-league debut? *(Answer on page 57.)*

28 In which year were Red Sox batters shut out by the opposition the fewest times? *(Answer on page 57.)*

29 Talk about demoralizing. Three times a Red Sox pitcher lost a no-hitter after working 8 2/3 innings. Only one out stood between these three pitchers and a no-hitter. Chances are you can name at least one of the three. Can you name all three? *(Answer on page 57.)*

30 True or false: Both Pedro Martinez and Roger Clemens threw a no-hitter in both the American and National Leagues, Pedro with the Expos and Red Sox, and Clemens for the Red Sox and Astros. *(Answer on page 58.)*

31 A double-barreled threat? This Red Sox reliever led the league in saves one year, got three starts the next year, and threw a no-hitter within 18 months of his leading the league in saves. Who was he? *(Answer on page 58.)*

32 Which Sox pitcher recorded the most wins in a row to kick off a season? This pitcher won, and then won again, and again, and ran his record to 14–0 before losing his first game. *(Answer on page 59.)*

33 Ten Red Sox players have recorded either a win or a loss in an All-Star Game. Can you identify the four who have won their games? *(Answer on page 59.)*
   A. Josh Beckett
   B. Roger Clemens
   C. Dennis Eckersley
   D. Lefty Grove
   E. Tex Hughson
   F. Pedro Martinez

G. Bill Monbouquette
H. Jonathan Papelbon
I. Dick Radatz
J. Frank Sullivan
K. Luis Tiant

34 We've seen earlier in this book how truly great a pitcher Babe Ruth was, winning 23 games one year for the Red Sox and 24 the next. He led the league in ERA and shutouts the year he won 23. Later in his career, he was an All-Star for the New York Yankees as a hitter, but why was he never named to an All-Star squad as a pitcher? *(Answer on page 60.)*

35 Frank Castillo was a member of the 2004 World Champion Boston Red Sox—with a 0.00 ERA for the entire season. If you don't remember him on that team, you may be forgiven. He only worked one inning, two-thirds of an inning on April 15 and one-third of an inning on April 18. In August 2002, he did something quite unusual. Maybe you can remember what he did? He probably wishes he hadn't. *(Answer on page 60.)*

36 What pitcher who worked 1,000 innings or more holds the lowest career ERA for the Red Sox? *(Answer on page 60.)*

37 Sixteen pitchers in major-league history have 3,000 or more strikeouts in their career. One of them is Pedro Martinez. What sole distinction, related to the 3,000 Ks, does Pedro hold? *(Answer on page 60.)*

38 Of all those 16 pitchers, who are the only two who have not yet been elected to the National Baseball Hall of Fame? *(Answer on page 61.)*

39 WHIP = walks and hits per inning pitched. With a minimum of 40 innings pitched, which pitcher (it's a Red Sox pitcher) has the lowest single-season WHIP in major-league history? *(Answer on page 61.)*

40 What about for a full season (minimum 162 innings)? Who has the best WHIP since at least the year 1901? *(Answer on page 61.)*

41 Which Red Sox pitcher holds the franchise record for most walks in a season by a left-hander and also holds the franchise record for most wins in a season by a left-hander? It was the same season. Hint: It was a left-hander. *(Answer on page 61.)*

42 Earl Wilson threw a no-hitter at Fenway Park on June 26, 1962—but he did more than that. What else did Wilson do that day? *(Answer on page 62.)*

43 The Monster—who was he? (Pretty easy question.) What might be the most remarkable stat about him? *(Answer on page 62.)*

44 Can you name two pitchers enshrined in the National Baseball Hall of Fame who were both 20-game losers for the Olde Towne Team? *(Answer on page 62.)*

45 For a pitcher to win 20 games in a season is quite rare. To have two 20-game winners on the same team in one season is much rarer. Has any Red Sox team ever had two 20-game winners in a given season? Yeah, probably, you're thinking, or why would we pose the question. OK, you're right about that part of it. But when was the last time the Red Sox had two 20-game winners on the same team? *(Answer on page 63.)*

46 Keeping the number 20 in mind, which pitcher (who has at least 20 career decisions) had the best career record (winning percentage) of any pitcher against the New York Yankees? *(Answer on page 64.)*

47 Home-run-hitting pitchers? OK, for an American League team, you're talking the old days (before 1973). Which Red Sox pitcher hit not just one, but two home runs and won his own game, driving in every run scored in the game? *(Answer on page 64.)*

48 This seems almost impossible. Which Red Sox player led the American League in earned run average one year and then—still with the Red Sox—won the home run crown just two years later? He's the only player in history to win both an ERA title and a batting crown. The batting crown was for another team. *(Answer on page 64.)*

49 Pitching and RBIs. Which Red Sox pitcher drove in more runs, in games he pitched, than any others? *(Answer on page 64.)*

50 Who was the last Red Sox pitcher to hit safely before the DH was instituted? *(Answer on page 64.)*

51 When was the last time a piece of excrement pitched for the Red Sox? *(Answer on page 65.)*

PITCHING ANSWERS

1 They all fit. In that sequence. The list presents the top 10 Red Sox pitchers, ranked in terms of wins for the Red Sox.
Roger Clemens: 192 wins
Cy Young: 192
Tim Wakefield: 186
Mel Parnell: 123
Luis Tiant: 122
Pedro Martinez: 116

Bill Monbouquette and Lefty Grove

Joe Wood: 115
Bob Stanley: 115
Jon Lester: 110
Joe Dobson: 106

The only other pitcher with 100 or more wins was Lefty Grove (105).

2 Young, as noted, threw 275 complete games in his eight seasons with Boston (1901–08). Two teammates rank second and third on the all-time list: Bill Dinneen (156 CG, from 1902–07) and George Winter (141 CG, 1901–08). Smoky Joe Wood (121) and Lefty Grove (119) round out the top five. Luis Tiant tied with Marvelous Mel Parnell at 113 complete games. Roger Clemens threw exactly 100. Pedro Martinez pitched 22. Even Babe Ruth topped Roger Clemens, with 105 complete games for the Red Sox. However, Clemens threw 18 complete games in the 1987 season, and no pitcher in either league has thrown that many since then.

Relievers? Who needs relievers? In 1904, the Young/Dinneen/Winter combination helped Boston throw 148 complete games of the 157 games played that year.

Note: Todd Anton never played for the Red Sox.

3 Bob Stanley pitched in 637 games for the Red Sox, the only big-league team for which he ever pitched. In 1977, he worked in 41 games, and in 1989 he worked in 43 games. In 1979 and 1987—just those two years—he worked primarily as a starter and even threw nine complete games in 1979. All in all, he started 85 of the 637 games. The pitcher who is #2 on the list is Tim Wakefield, with 590 games (he pitched 37 games for the Pirates before coming to Boston—though he started as a first baseman for Pittsburgh). Some 430 of Wake's 590 games were starts, in a Red Sox career that ran from 1995 through 2011. Number 3 is Jonathan Papelbon, much further back, with 396 appearances, all except three of them in relief.

4 If you were paying sufficient attention to the answer to the prior question, you would know it could be none other than Tim Wakefield, who started those 430 games. Number 2 on the list is Roger Clemens (382), with Cy Young's 287 placing him third.

Tim Wakefield on the mound.

5 Pedro! Pedro Martinez, that is. One hundred—that's a lot of decisions. Bob Stanley, who we saw appeared in 637 games, got there with room to spare. So did Tim Wakefield. But Jonathan Papelbon, #3 on the list of appearances, only had 42 (he was 23–19, but with an excellent 2.33 ERA over the course of his seven seasons with the Sox. He saved 219 games, and—while not "decisions"—that's pretty important. Pedro Martinez was 117–37 with the Red Sox, for a winning percentage of .760. Smoky Joe Wood ranks second, with a .674 winning percentage. And we suspect most people wouldn't accurately pick the #3 guy. It was Babe Ruth—his 89–46 record with the Red Sox gives him a .659 winning percentage.

6 It was Hideo Nomo, and it wasn't actually that long ago. He pitched for 5 1/3 innings, giving up three runs, and lost to the Yankees in New York on Sunday afternoon, September 9, 2001. Less than 48 hours later, on September 11, Al-Qaeda terrorists wreaked their havoc, with two of the hijacked airplanes taking down the two World Trade Center towers in New York City. Air travel was shut down for some days, and, out of respect as well as practicality, there was no baseball played for a full week. When it was time to start playing again, the Red Sox were at Fenway Park, hosting Tampa Bay on September 18. It was their first game after the game of September 9. Nomo started and won that game, working seven full innings, 7–2. The game he had lost nine days earlier was a 7–2 loss.

7 That is Red Ruffing, who was 10–25 for the Red Sox in 1928. In 1929, he was 9–22 and led the American League in losses yet again. In the course of seven seasons, he was 39–96 for the Red Sox. So how'd he get into the Hall of Fame? He was traded to the New York Yankees in May of 1930 and was 231–124 (with a 7–2 record in the World Series) for them.

8 To lead your league in wins, strikeouts, and earned run average is pitching's Triple Crown. Boston has only had two, and they more or less bracketed the twentieth century. Cy Young achieved the feat in 1901 and Pedro Martinez did it in 1999. The very first year of the franchise, after eleven years in the National League, Cy Young was enticed over to join the Boston Americans. He already held a career mark of 286–170. He was coming off a 19–19 year with the St. Louis Cardinals but posted an outstanding 33–10 mark for Boston, with a 1.62 ERA aided by his 158 strikeouts. Young had 41 starts and threw 38 complete games. He relieved two times. In every game he appeared in, he was credited with a win or a loss. He had seven more wins than the second-place finisher, 31 more strikeouts, and the next-closest ERA was almost a full run higher: 2.42. He held batters to an opponents' batting average of .232 and on-base percentage of just .256.

The next Red Sox pitcher to win the Triple Crown was Pedro Martinez, who did so in 1999. Pedro struck out almost twice as many batters as had Cy, whiffing 313. He had an astonishing year, relative to other pitchers in the league. His 23 wins were five more than the second-winningest pitcher, Cleveland's Bartolo Colon. His 313 strikeouts were more than 100 above the #2 man, Chuck Finley, who struck out an even 200 opponents. His ERA of 2.07 was more than a run higher than David Cone of the Yankees, who finished second with 3.44. He posted a strikeouts-to-walks ratio of 8.46; the next closest wasn't even half that, at 3.44 (Felix Heredia). He struck out an average of 13.20 batters per nine innings. Finley came the closest: 8.44. His WHIP (walks plus hits per innings pitched) was .923. Eric Milton's 1.226 was as close as anyone approached Pedro that year.—from *Red Sox Threads*

9 Here he is again, the same guy who popped up three questions ago! It was Hideo Nomo, and it was Wednesday night, April 4, 2001, at Camden Yards in Baltimore. He walked three but held the Orioles hitless in his first game wearing a Red Sox uniform. The Sox won, 3–0, the game-winning hit being Brian Daubach's two-run homer in the top of the third inning. For Nomo, this was his second no-hitter. As a member of the Los Angeles Dodgers, he threw a no-hitter against the Rockies at Coors Field back on September 17, 1996. Now he had a no-hitter in each league.

Buchholz's no-hitter came in his second start. Parnell's no-hitter only came in his final year with the Red Sox.

10 Howard Ehmke did this on September 7, 1923. As Gregory H. Wolf explained, the opposing pitcher on the Philadelphia Athletics, Slim Harriss, lined a double to left field in the sixth inning. The umpires ruled he had failed to touch first base, so he was out and the base hit was erased. Later in the game, Frank Welch lined to

Mike Menosky in left. Menosky fumbled the ball. Initially ruled a hit, the official scorer changed it to an error.

11 True. He pitched to 76 consecutive batters without giving up a hit, in 1904, spanning 25 1/3 hitless innings. It was part of a run in which he threw 45 2/3 scoreless innings in a row (which included four shutouts in a row). And while we're gasping, three of the shutouts were 1–0 ballgames. Young was 26–16 that year.

12 Koji Uehara, in 2013, ninety-six years after Shore's feat. Uehara retired 37 consecutive batters from August 17, 2013, to September 13, 2013. Of the 37 batters he set down, one after the other, 17 of them were by strikeouts.

13 They are Lou Criger, Bill Carrigan, Bob Tillman, and Jason Varitek.

Criger caught these three no-hitters:

Cy Young: May 5, 1904 (perfect game)
Bill Dinneen: September 27, 1905
Cy Young: June 30, 1908

Bill Carrigan, who was also the manager of the Red Sox from 1913–16 and 1927–29, also caught three no-hitters, two of them while serving as manager:

Joe Wood: July 29, 1911
Rube Foster: June 21, 1916
Dutch Leonard: August 30, 1916

Bob Tillman, who was Red Sox catcher from 1962 until the Sox sold him to the Yankees in early August 1967, caught two no-hitters:

Earl Wilson: June 26, 1962
Dave Morehead: September 16, 1965

And Jason Varitek holds the major-league record for no-hitters caught, with four (really, five):

Hideo Nomo: April 4, 2001
Derek Lowe: April 27, 2002

Devern Hansack: October 1, 2006*
Clay Buchholz: September 1, 2007
Jon Lester: May 19, 2008

*That's five. But you said four and then added "really, five." What's going on here?

Major League Baseball declines to credit Devern with an official no-hitter. On October 1, 2006, Varitek caught Devern Hansack when the Nicaraguan right-hander faced the Baltimore Orioles at Fenway Park in the very last game of the season. The game was called after five full innings, due to rain. One team had been hitting; the other had not. Kicked off by a three-run Mike Lowell homer in the bottom of the first inning, the Red Sox had amassed nine runs on seven hits and two Orioles errors. Hansack had not allowed the Orioles any hits. He'd walked one, in the top of the second, though he was erased on a double play.

With five innings having been played, it was an official game. You'll find it even today in the books as a shutout and a complete game, with no hits. But, according to an amendment in baseball's rules in 1991, "An official no-hit game occurs when a pitcher (or pitchers) allows no hits during the entire course of a game, which consists of at least nine innings." So, by this new rule, Hansack had a no-hitter (that much is obvious, given that there were no hits and he was credited with a complete game), but it is not deemed an "official" no-hit game.

14 This may actually have happened more than once, but here's the one we know. It was April 21, 1946, at Fenway Park. The Philadelphia Athletics were in town for a doubleheader. Boston won the first game, 12–11, in 10 innings—thanks to a six-run Red Sox rally in the bottom of the ninth, and then Ted Williams singling in relief pitcher Joe Dobson in the bottom of the 10th. Jim Bagby Jr. started the second game. He walked leadoff batter Elmer Valo. Then he walked Hal Peck. Shortstop Jack Wallaesa walked to the plate, and Bagby gave him a base on balls, too. The bases were loaded, with nobody out, and yet no Athletics batter had an official at-bat. There was no place to put center fielder Sam Chapman, but Bagby walked him anyhow. Finally, manager Joe Cronin concluded this wasn't Bagby's day. Randy Heflin was asked to relieve. Not one of the three inherited runners bestowed upon Heflin scored. He secured one out and then induced a double play to get out of the inning. But it was 1–0, Athletics, and the Red Sox never scored (they were held to three hits off Bobo Newsom, two of them by Dom DiMaggio), so Bagby was tagged with the loss.

15 He is Matt Young. What's a no-hitter if that isn't it? Check the box score of April 14, 1992—the first game of a doubleheader in Cleveland. The Indians scored once in the bottom of the first on a walk, a stolen base, and an error. They scored again in the bottom of the third on two walks, a stolen base, and a fielder's choice. The Red Sox scored once, in the top of the fourth. Neither team scored again nor did any Indians player ever get a base hit. The score remained 2–1 in favor of the Indians through eight innings. When the Sox failed to score in the top of the ninth, the game was over. There was no point to Cleveland batting again; they'd already won the game—even though they never had a hit. Young, who averaged 6.48 strikeouts per game in his 10-year career, had struck out six in this game. This was not his best game; he walked seven Indians batters. The Red Sox had left 11 men on base, but only scored the one run, so Young—who hadn't allowed even one base hit—lost the game.

A committee appointed by the Commissioner had ruled—just the year before, in 1991—that you have to pitch nine innings to be credited with a no-hitter, and, since Cleveland didn't bat in the bottom of the ninth (having already won the game), Young was deprived of the credit for an "official" no-hitter. The committee no doubt had in mind the game thrown by the Yankees' Andy Hawkins on July 1, 1990, which he lost against the White Sox, 4–0.

April 14, 1992, was not a good day for Cleveland batters. In the second game of the doubleheader, Roger Clemens went the distance against them and won a 3–0 two-hitter. He walked three and struck out 12. When the Indians went home at day's end, they'd won one and lost one but had only had two hits in the combined games of the doubleheader.

16 Tim Wakefield. In a game in Detroit on August 8, 2004, Wakefield allowed six home runs. Most times, of course, a manager would have removed the pitcher after four home runs. Not manager Terry Francona in this game. Wake gave up a homer to Ivan Rodriguez in the first inning, but then Boston scored twice in the second. Wakefield surrendered two solo homers in the bottom of the second (Craig Monroe and Eric Munson), but that only made the score 3–2, and Kevin Youkilis homered to lead off the Boston third.

Rodriguez homered again in the Tigers' third, and so did Carlos Pena. It was now 6–3 Tigers, but then the Red Sox scored six runs in the top of the fourth. In the fifth inning, Detroit first baseman Dmitri Young hit another Tiger homer—#6 of the game, in five innings. With a 10–7 lead, Francona relieved Wakefield after five innings. Why court disaster any longer? The move worked, and Wakefield won the game, the final being 11–9. (There was another home run in the game; Munson collected a second home run, too, off Mike Timlin in the eighth inning.)

17 Rich Hill, one of the relatively few natives of the City of Boston to ever play for the Red Sox. He'd been a reliever

in 2010, 2011, and 2012 for the Red Sox. He'd gone elsewhere but came back to the Sox in September 2015 and started four games. In the first three, he struck out 10 batters in each game. In the same hundred years, there is only one other Red Sox pitcher who ever struck out 10 or more batters in three consecutive games, with one or fewer walks each game: Pedro Martinez (August 19–30, 1999).

18 This wasn't one of those anomalous wonders who does something amazing and then is barely heard of again. The pitcher was Pedro Martinez. It was a Saturday afternoon game against the Seattle Mariners on May 18, 2002. It was 41 degrees, windy, and wet. As Michael Holley wrote in the next day's *Boston Globe*, "Martinez's first pitch was a strike. His second pitch was a strike. So was his third. So were the next six. Nine pitches, nine strikes, three outs. He made Ichiro Suzuki, Mark McLemore, and Ruben Sierra look like kids who just arrived from Tacoma. He was on his game, theoretically competing with the Mariners but realistically trying to outdo himself." McLemore was called out on strikes; Suzuki and Sierra went down swinging. Pedro went eight innings, and Urbina pitched the ninth. Pedro struck out six more Mariners, and he allowed six hits; the Sox won the game, 4–1. And he remains the only pitcher in league history ever to have opened a game with three straight strikeouts on nine pitches.

He's not the only pitcher to strike out the side on nine pitches in an inning; Lefty Grove did that twice in 1928, with the Athletics, and it's been done by others. But he's the first and only one to have done it to open a game.

19 It's Pedro Martinez again. In the 1999 season, he averaged 13.2 batters struck out for every nine innings pitched. That same year, he set a franchise record with 313 Ks. He also won his second Cy Young Award. He'd won a Cy for the Expos in 1997, so he had proven dominance in both leagues. He won another Cy Young Award for the Red Sox the very next year, 2000. That year he "only" whiffed 11.8 batters per nine innings (with 284 strikeouts), but that was enough to lead the league again in both categories. And win his third Cy Young. Roger Clemens, Randy Johnson, and Gaylord Perry are the only three other pitchers to have won a Cy in both leagues.

20 It was not Pedro Martinez. Nope, it was teammate Tim Wakefield who struck out four batters in the bottom of the ninth inning in a game at Kauffman Stadium in Kansas City on August 10, 1999. Three Red Sox pitchers had combined to hold the Royals to three runs, and the Sox were leading, 5–3. Wakefield struck out Chad Kreuter looking for the first out of the inning. Then he got pinch-hitter Scott Pose swinging. The Royals were down to their final out. Johnny Damon came up to bat for Kansas City, and he struck out, too (also, a swinging strike)—but Sox catcher Jason Varitek missed the ball. It got away from him, a passed ball.

Had Varitek held onto the ball, the game would have been over. Instead, it suddenly became "white-knuckle time"—Damon ran to first base and reached safely. Carlos Febles came to bat, and another passed ball allowed Damon to take second. That became a moot point of sorts when Febles hit a game-tying two-run homer to left field. Wakefield then struck out Carlos Beltran to end the inning, but the score was now 5–5. "Nothing I could do about it," Wakefield said after the game. "I was throwing strikes, I struck out four guys in an inning, and Febles hit a great pitch."

The Red Sox didn't waste time and scored four runs in the top of the 10th inning. In the bottom of the 10th, Wakefield took the mound again. He secured one out, gave up a double to Jermaine Dye, and then struck out Joe Randa. Jeremy Giambi doubled, driving in Dye. Wakefield then faced Chad Kreuter again for the second time in two innings and struck him out again for the third out. But, once more, the ball got away from Varitek—another passed ball on a pitch that otherwise would have ended the game. Kreuter reached first base and Giambi ran to third. Improbable as it was, the tying run was now at the plate in the person of Jed Hansen. Rather than take too many chances, Sox manager Jimy Williams called on Rich Garces to relive Wakefield. Garces struck out Hansen. Tek held the ball. Wake won the game.

21 It was his last game for the Red Sox. He was a veteran pitcher, Ken Chase, and it was on Sunday, June 13, 1943, in the first game of a Fenway doubleheader. He came on in relief, inheriting some runners, who scored. The three earlier Sox pitchers were charged with 10 runs. Chase worked the final four innings, giving up four hits and six more runs. He faced 27 batters, walking the aforesaid 11 men, while striking out one.

22 It didn't happen until 1984. During the August 9 night game at Arlington Stadium, right-hander and Tennessean Charlie Mitchell, age 22, came in to pitch the bottom of the eighth inning. The Rangers had a 6–3 lead. The first Ranger up was their first baseman, Pete O'Brien, who homered. Mitchell then retired the next three batters on two groundouts and a fly ball to center. The homer was one of only two home runs Mitchell ever surrendered—though he only pitched 18 big-league innings. After the game, manager Ralph Houk told the *Boston Herald*, "It's a tough thing for someone pitching in their first big league game. But he showed me something the way his fastball was down and sinking on the next three hitters."

Jeff Suppan pitched 2,542 2/3 major-league innings over 17 seasons. But the first batter he faced was Kansas City second baseman Keith Lockhart on July 17, 1995, at Fenway Park. A line-drive home run to deep right field. Suppan got out of the inning and pitched 5 2/3 innings in all but bore the loss as the Royals won the game, 4–3, their margin of victory being that leadoff solo home run.

On Opening Day, April 2, 2007 (a good year for the Red Sox overall), Hideki Okajima took over in relief in the bottom of the sixth inning. The very first pitch he threw in the majors was to Kansas City catcher John Buck—who drove it out of the park to deep center field. He got the next three batters, but the Royals already had a 5–1 lead before Oki's pitch. They won in the end, 7–1. "I was pretty shocked," said Okajima after the game, though he said he'd thrown the pitch where he had wanted to.

The 2007 banner on Yawkey Way.

Gordon Edes of the *Globe* then said he amended that: "Maybe not exactly where I wanted to throw it."

23 It wasn't three. It wasn't four. It was eight different pitchers. Eight! It was the last day of the 1999 season, October 3, at Camden Yards, and the Sox were headed to the playoffs as the wild card team. Maybe manager Jimy Williams wanted to spread the work around and give everyone a taste. The Sox pitchers, in the order they worked, were Pat Rapp, Rheal Cormier, Rich Garces, Derek Lowe, Tom Gordon, Rod Beck, Brian Rose, and Tim Wakefield. It was a game filled with some animosity, with three hit batsmen, a bat flung toward the mound by Troy O'Leary, the same bat flung back at the Red Sox as the benches emptied. Batter and pitcher were ejected.

The melee was in the fourth inning. The Red Sox didn't get their first base hit until after 7 2/3 innings. The score was 0–0 at the time, and still the score after nine full innings. In the top of the 10th, facing Orioles reliever Mike Timlin, the Sox scored a run on three singles. The two Sox pitchers who worked more than one inning (no one worked a partial inning) were starter Rapp and reliever Rose, who worked the eighth and ninth and got the win after Wakefield held Baltimore scoreless in the bottom of the 10th.

The Tampa Bay Rays equaled the eight-pitcher record in October 2010.

24 It's been one hundred years. In the 1916 season, Mr. George Herman "Babe" Ruth threw nine shutouts. He was 23–12 on the season with a 1.75 earned run average. It was a good year for Sox shutouts; Dutch Leonard also threw six. The team as a whole shut out the opposition 23 times. Ernie Shore and Rube Foster each threw three shutouts, and Carl Mays threw two. And Leonard and Mays combined to shut out the St. Louis Browns for 17 innings on July 14. The game ended in a 0–0 tie.

Ruth spread the whitewash around a little. He shut out the Tigers three times, the Yankees twice, Washington twice, and Cleveland twice. The Athletics and White Sox emerged unscathed. Three of Ruth's shutouts were 1–0 wins.

Ruth had 17 shutouts in the course of his 158 games pitched for the Boston Red Sox.

25 Ray Culp (1968) and Luis Tiant (1972), and Cy Young, way back in 1903. Culp threw 39 scoreless innings in a row and improved on that, to 42 1/3 consecutive innings of scoreless ball. Three of Cy Young's shutouts—three in a row—were 1–0 games. Culp's shutouts were on September 13, 17, 21, and 25, with 16 hits surrendered over the four games. Tiant's shutouts were on August 19, 25, 29, and September 4, and he, too, surrendered a total of 16 base hits in his four shutout games.

26 Perhaps a surprise. There are two, and they are tied. Both Cy Young and Roger Clemens are tied for the most wins as a Red Sox pitcher—with 192 wins apiece. They also tied in shutouts. Both pitchers threw 38 shutouts for the Red Sox. Over the course of his career, Young threw 76 shutouts. Clemens threw 46.

27 See how you did. Here are the seven:

Rube Kroh: September 30, 1906

Larry Pape: July 6, 1909

Buck O'Brien: September 9, 1911

George Hockette: September 17, 1934

Dave "Boo" Ferriss: April 29, 1945

Dave Morehead: April 13, 1963

Billy Rohr: April 14, 1967

Obviously, it's been about half a century since anyone has done it.

28 One might have thought it was 1950. But it wasn't. It was 1995. The Sox were shut out just one time all season long. Contrast that to 1906, when they were shut out 28 times—in a shorter season. Unsurprisingly, the Red Sox finished higher in the standings in 1995 than they did in 1906. Quite a bit higher. Sox pitchers threw nine shutouts in '95, but the only time the team was shut out was on August 2, in Detroit. The winning pitcher, who went the distance, was the immortal Sean Bergman, during a 7–10 season. The losing pitcher was Roger Clemens, losing on back-to-back homers in the bottom of the fifth. There was one close play, when Boston almost scored in the top of the sixth, but Lee Tinsley was thrown out at the plate.

29 Interestingly, every one of the three times came in a year when the Red Sox won the American League pennant. The first one was Billy Rohr (April 14, 1967) against the Yankees. That's the one we're going to guess most people got. The player who broke up the no-hitter was

Elston Howard—who became a member of the Red Sox before the year was done. Next was Rick Wise (July 2, 1975). After getting those first two outs, he walked a batter and then gave up a two-run homer to the Brewers' George Scott. Oops. No-hitter gone. Shutout gone. Fortunately, the Red Sox had a 6–0 lead before Boomer's homer. Then Wise gave up another home run to the next batter, Bobby Darwin. Finally, he secured the elusive third out. He won the game, 6–3, a two-hitter. Curt Schilling was the third of our three pitchers. He was pitching for the Red Sox at Oakland on June 7, 2007. Eight innings of no-hit pitching. Then a groundout, and another groundout. He'd struck out four and walked no one, the only thing between him and a perfect game being a fifth-inning error by Julio Lugo. A single to short right field off the bat of Shannon Stewart spoiled the no-hitter. Schill retired the last batter on a foul popup.

30 Totally false. Neither pitcher ever threw a no-hitter in either the American League or the National League. They've earned many other honors, but neither ever threw a no-hitter. There was a brilliant one-hitter that Pedro once threw, on September 10, 1999, at Yankee Stadium. He struck out 17 batters, including eight of the last nine batters he faced. The one hit was a Chili Davis solo home run in the bottom of the second inning. He then retired the next 22 batters in order.

31 They called him D-Lowe. Derek Lowe led the league with 42 saves in 2000 (working as a closer, he finished a league-leading 64 games). In 2001, he appeared in 67 games (three of them starts) and then threw a no-hitter against the visiting Tampa Bay Devil Rays (they hadn't dropped the "Devil" yet) on April 27, 2002, at Fenway Park. It was an efficient 97-pitch win. He struck out six and walked only one Ray, way back in the third inning. The seven runs the Red Sox scored in the bottom of the third inning gave him a cushion of comfort.

32 That was the Rocket, Roger Clemens, kicking off the 1986 season. He was 7–5 in 1985. Come 1986, he was—apparently—more than ready. Clemens didn't lose a game in April (4–0), nor in May (when he improved to 8–0), nor in June (when six wins in one month bumped it up to 14–0). After the first half of the season, Clemens's record was 14–0. On July 2, he lost his first game. The Red Sox were ahead after seven innings, 2–1. But when he gave up one run and had put two more on base, manager John McNamara called on Bob Stanley in relief. Both inherited runners scored, and the loss was rightly attributed to Clemens. That was his first loss. He lost his next start, too, a two-game losing streak. Clemens finished the season 24–4 and won the first of his unrivaled seven Cy Young Awards.

33 Roger Clemens: 1986
Pedro Martinez: 1999
Josh Beckett: 2007
Jonathan Papelbon: 2006

That's right. Every one of the first six Sox pitchers to get a decision drew a loss. Then the next four all earned wins.

34 You can't fault the voters for any oversight. The first All-Star Game was not held until 1933. Babe Ruth's big years as a pitcher were 1915 and 1916. His work helped get the Red Sox into two World Series, both of which they won, but there simply was no All-Star squad to which he could have been selected.

35 He pitched for a cycle, sort of. In fact, it was about the worst sort of cycle you could imagine. During a season when he was 6–15 for the Red Sox, he pitched against the Texas Rangers at The Ballpark in Arlington on August 1, 2002. He gave up 10 runs but didn't get the loss. That's because it was assigned to starter John Burkett, who gave up eight. The Sox lost, 19–7. Castillo came on in the bottom of the second and gave up two walks sandwiched around a single, and then a grand slam to Carl Everett. In the bottom of the third, he gave up a solo home run to Kevin Mench. And later that same inning, a three-run homer to Todd Hollandsworth. In the fifth inning, it was a two-run homer to Mike Lamb. So, a one-run homer, a two-run homer, a three-run homer, and a grand slam.

36 Smoky Joe Wood, whose Red Sox career ERA of 1.99 just edges out Cy Young's 2.00. Third on the list is Dutch Leonard at 2.13, and fourth is Babe Ruth, with a Red Sox career ERA of 2.19.

37 He's the only one to strike out 3,000 or more batters in fewer than 3,000 innings. (In other words, he struck out more than one batter per inning throughout his entire career.) In all, Pedro struck out 3,124 batters in 2,827 1/3 innings—basically, an average of 10 strikeouts per nine innings. Randy Johnson struck out 10.6 batters per innings, for a total of 4,875 Ks, in 4,135 1/3 innings.

38 Roger Clemens and Curt Schilling.

39 Koji Uehara, in 2013. He had a WHIP of 0.57. There are Red Sox connections of one sort or another with the pitchers ranked #2, #3, and #4. They are Dennis Eckersley (with Oakland in 1987): 0.61. And Dennis Eckersley (with Oakland in 1990), also 0.61. And Craig Kimbrel with Atlanta in 2012 (0.65).

40 Pedro Martinez, in the year 2000, had a WHIP of 0.737. That stands as the major-league record since the year 1900. He threw 217 innings and led the league with 284 strikeouts (while walking only 32 batters). He hit 14 batters and gave up 128 base hits. His 1.75 earned run average that year led the major leagues (one of five years he led the majors in ERA). There were six years in which he led in WHIP. The #2 WHIP pitcher in 2000 was the Yankees' Mike Mussina, with 1.187.

41 Mel Parnell, in 1949. He was 25–7 that year, leading the majors in wins. His 2.77 ERA led the American League. His 134 walks is the all-time single-season record for a Red Sox lefty. And the 25 wins is the most ever recorded by a Red Sox southpaw in a given year. If he'd only been given the ball to pitch in the single-game playoff for the pennant against Cleveland. But, no, manager Joe McCarthy gave the ball to Denny Galehouse instead.

42 Wilson's bat won the game; his solo homer in the third inning off the Los Angeles Angels' Bo Belinsky was all the scoring that was needed to win the game. The final was a 2–0 win. Boston had added a second run in the fourth inning. Belinsky only allowed three hits in seven innings of work. Wilson's win was the first no-hitter by a Red Sox right-hander since Howard Ehmke had thrown one in 1923.

43 The Monster was Dick Radatz. He was 6-foot-6 and listed at 230 pounds, but somehow he seemed bigger than that. He apparently didn't like the nickname, but it wasn't one he ever had any chance of escaping. Radatz won 15 games in 1963 and 16 games in 1964—as a relief pitcher. In 1963, only Bill Monbouqette won more games for the Red Sox (Monbo was 20–10), but Radatz had a 1.97 ERA compared to Monbouquette's 3.81. In 1964, Radatz appeared in 67 games, threw 157 innings, and had more wins than any pitcher on the Sox staff. Monbouquette was second with 13 wins. On top of the wins, Radatz had 29 saves—enough to lead both leagues.

44 In 1906, despite a decent 3.19 ERA, Cy Young was a 20-game loser with a record of 13–21.

In the nineteenth century, he'd twice lost more than 20 games for Cleveland. And, not that many questions earlier in this very book, we pointed out that Red Ruffing was 10–25 in 1928 (3.89 ERA) and 9–22 in 1929

L to R: Herb Pennock, Doc Cramer, and Moe Berg.

(4.86 ERA). Herb Pennock had flirted with it in 1922; he lost 17 games. Cy Young was inducted into the Hall of Fame in 1937, receiving a reported 153 of 201 ballots. That's 76 percent of the vote. He just squeaked in. This does make you wonder: what were those other 48 voters thinking? Thirty years later, Red Ruffing was inducted in 1967 by the BBWAA in a "runoff election," with 266 of 306 ballots.

45 It wasn't all that long ago. In 2002, the Red Sox had Derek Lowe, who was 21–8 (2.58 ERA), and Pedro Martinez, who was 20–4 (2.26). That's a combined total of—easy math—41–12 for the two pitchers. John Burkett won 13 that year, and Tim Wakefield won 11. No one else won more than six.

46 In his career as a whole, Babe Ruth was 17–5 against the Yankees. Even better, he was 20–5 against the St. Louis Browns. There was no team against which he had a losing record.

47 The pitcher was Sonny Siebert. The date was September 2, 1971. The place was Fenway Park. The Baltimore Orioles were in town. Siebert shut out the O's on three hits. In the bottom of the third inning, he hit a solo home run off opposing pitcher Pat Dobson. With two outs in the bottom of the fifth, Duane Josephson singled. Then Siebert hit a two-run shot. He hit 12 homers in his major-league pitching career.

48 This was none other than Babe Ruth. His 1.75 ERA went with a 23–12 record and led the AL in 1916. Two years later, in 1918, his 11 home runs led the leagues, and not just among pitchers. He led *all* batters in the league. It was obviously not a homer-heavy year. In 1919, he homered 29 times, again leading the league, and drove in 113 runs, also tops in the league.

49 Babe Ruth drove in 61 runs in 1918 and 113 runs in 1919, but not in games he pitched. He drove in about a dozen runs as a pitcher in 1918 and nine or so in 1919 (as RBIs were not an official statistic at the time). The answer to the question is Wes Ferrell, in 1935. He drove in 24 runs as a pitcher and another eight as a pinch-hitter.

50 The designated hitter was instituted in the American League beginning with the 1973 season. The last pitcher to get a base hit before the DH came in was Luis Tiant. On October 3, 1972, Tiant singled off Woodie Fryman of the Tigers in the top of the seventh. This is not to say that pitchers haven't hit safely since. Of course, with interleague play, there are still times when AL pitchers come to bat.

And it's not just then. Occasionally, things happen. For instance, take the game where the Red Sox played the Mariners on May 22, 1996, at Fenway Park. Norm Charlton was pitching for Seattle, and in the bottom of the eighth inning, Roger Clemens came up to bat. He singled right up the middle. As Dan Shaughnessy of the *Boston Globe* wrote, "The situation developed when Kevin Kennedy managed himself out of the designated hitter. Clemens was inserted into the ninth spot in the order after the Sox batted around in the seventh."

"Norm has that big leg kick," noted Clemens. "I was trying to pick the ball up. I just threw the head of the bat out there and I was fortunate. I think Norm was as surprised as I was.

"A laughing [José] Canseco said, 'We were all up in the dugout saying, "God, is it that easy to hit in this league?"'" Clemens did bat 1.000 on the season.

51 From the book *Curse in the Rearview Mirror*. Clearly, this is a matter of opinion and some fans wouldn't dig deeply to suggest a date, but writer Bill Ballou has documentary evidence that it was August 12, 1956, at Griffith Stadium in Washington, DC. Right-hander Tommy Hurd came into the game to pitch the fifth and sixth, surrendering four runs. Most box scores show him correctly as Hurd, but the one Bill has in his scrapbook couldn't be any clearer: Turd.

Opening Week at Fenway Park, April 2011.

5

HITTING

With the cluster of pitchers who were hitters, we've already started the transition from pitching to hitting. Let's look now at Boston batters.

1 Ted Williams broke into the major leagues at the age of 20 in 1939. He set two major-league rookie records that first season and still holds both of them. What are Ted's two rookie records? *(Answer on page 77.)*

2 Who holds the team record for the best batting average for a rookie? *(Answer on page 77.)*

3 Here's a good long list. Select which of the following Red Sox players hit home runs in their first game at Fenway Park. *(Answer on page 78.)*

A. Eddie Pellagrini

B. Butch Hobson

C. Darnell McDonald

D. Tony Conigliaro

E. Jim Rice

F. Curtis Pride

G. Ken Harrelson

H. Billy Rohr

I. Rob Deer

J. Rip Repulski

K. Bob Tillman

L. Daniel Nava

M. Wilfred Lefebvre

N. Lou Merloni

4 Let's get the Bill Buckner reference over with quickly. Bill Buckner's famous misplay happened at Shea Stadium during Game Six of the 1986 World Series. It's been played incessantly on television ever since. True Red Sox fans remember how Buckner played hard for a few years with bandaged, aching legs, and—contrary to media-stoked myth—he was never driven out of town. He played the full 1987 season, was welcomed back in 1990, and closed his career out with the Sox. Though not known as a home run hitter (the 18 homers he hit in 1986 were his career high), there was something quite remarkable about his very last home run for the Red Sox, hit at Fenway Park. What was it? *(Answer on page 79.)*

5 There was a year in which a Red Sox slugger led the major leagues in homers but hit every single one of them on the road—not a single homer in his home park in Boston, Fenway Park. Can you name him? *(Answer on page 79.)*

6 Which Red Sox player has won the most Silver Slugger Awards? *(Answer on page 79.)*

7 Outta the park! Hundreds of balls have been hit over the Green Monster. How many have been hit out of the park in straightaway center and how many in right field? *(Answer on page 79.)*

8 What is the longest home run ever hit at Fenway Park? *(Answer on page 80.)*

9 Hitting for the cycle (a single, a double, a triple, and a home run—all in the same game) is such a rare feat that among the thousands of players in the thousands of games in franchise history, it's only been done 20 times. Opponents have only done so 12 times against Boston pitchers. How many times have Fenway Park patrons seen a cycle hit by the home team? Extra credit if you can correctly guess the number of times Red Sox batters have hit a "natural cycle"—hitting a single, double, triple, and homer in that precise sequence—at home? *(Answer on page 81.)*

10 What's the closest anyone ever came to hitting for the cycle all in one inning? *(Answer on page 82.)*

11 On September 1, 1967, Ken Harrelson tripled in the first, homered in the fifth, and doubled in the seventh. Asked after the game what he would have done if he'd gotten another at-bat and hit a home run, what did he say? *(Answer on page 83.)*

12 Hitting for the cycle has only been done 21 times in Red Sox history. John Valentin hit for the cycle on June 6, 1996. Has anyone hit for one since? *(Answer on page 83.)*

13 Who was the most recent player in Red Sox history to hit an inside-the-park home run? *(Answer on page 84.)*

14 Did a switch-hitter ever win a batting title for the Red Sox? If so, can you name him? *(Answer on page 84.)*

15 RBIs. Which Red Sox batter drove in the most runs during a single season? *(Answer on page 84.)*

16 Which two among the following did NOT drive in 10 RBIs all in one game? *(Answer on page 85.)*
   A. Jimmie Foxx
   B. Ted Williams
   C. Norm Zauchin
   D. Nomar Garciaparra
   E. Fred Lynn
   F. Rudy York

17 Which former Red Sox player tied the legendary Sadaharu Oh for the most home runs by a player in a single season in Japanese professional baseball? *(Answer on page 85.)*

18 Ted Williams was the MVP in 1949. He hit 43 homers and drove in 159 runs. Both were career bests. That year, Ted had 368 total bases—his best season. It would clearly be a major accomplishment to record 400 total bases in one year. Who was the last player in the American League to achieve this, and when did he do it? *(Answer on page 86.)*

19 Is on-base percentage a better offensive stat than simple batting average? Which Red Sox player holds the major-league record for lifetime on-base percentage? *(Answer on page 86.)*

20 Now let's look simply at base hits in a single season. Which Red Sox batter had the most 200-hit seasons? *(Answer on page 88.)*

A. Ted Williams

B. Carl Yastrzemski

C. Jim Rice

D. Wade Boggs

E. Nomar Garciaparra

F. Johnny Pesky

21 Jim Rice won the American League MVP award in 1978, hit over .300 in seven seasons, and was an eight-time All-Star. He was named to the National Baseball Hall of Fame in 2009. Four years in a row, he led the major leagues in one particular stat, and he holds the major-league record in this statistic. What is it? *(Answer on page 88.)*

22 Which Red Sox player holds the record for extra-base hits in a game? *(Answer on page 88.)*

23 Which Red Sox player had the most 30-home-run seasons, with the Red Sox? *(Answer on page 88.)*

24 Ted Williams hit 521 home runs in his major-league career. It's one thing to hit a home run with nobody on base in the third inning of a "meaningless" game. As anyone who followed David Ortiz in the postseason can tell you, it's another thing to get a big hit in a big game. How many of The Kid's 521 homers were game-winning hits? *(Answer on page 88.)*

A. 9

B. 34

C. 52

D. 96

E. 520

25 David Ortiz set the Red Sox single-season record for home runs in 2006 when he homered 54 times (breaking Jimmie Foxx's record of 50, which Foxx had held since 1938). But Ortiz struck out 117 times, a little more than twice as many times as he homered. (Foxx had struck out 76 times in '38.) Was there ever a Red Sox slugger who hit more home runs than he made strikeouts? *(Answer on page 89.)*

26 Who holds the Major League record for reaching base safely in consecutive plate appearances? In other words, this player reached base via base hit or bases on balls (or being hit by a pitch) in X plate appearances in a row. *(Answer on page 89.)*

27 This is a whole other thing—reaching base safely at least once in consecutive games. Even casual baseball fans know that Joe DiMaggio had a 56-game hit streak. If you add walks and being perhaps hit by a pitch, which Red Sox player holds the major-league record for reaching base in consecutive games? Obviously, it's longer than Joe D's hitting streak. *(Answer on page 90.)*

28 One Red Sox player (hint: he was a member of the 1967 Impossible Dream Red Sox) had only one hit in his entire Red Sox career. We're excluding pitchers here. This was a position player. Who was it? *(Answer on page 90.)*

29 This Red Sox player never hit a grand slam throughout his entire Red Sox career—until his final season, when he hit four of them. Which one of these Sox sluggers was the one? *(Answer on page 90.)*

A. Mike Greenwell

B. Ted Williams

C. Jackie Jensen

D. Babe Ruth

E. Jimmie Foxx

F. Nomar Garciaparra

30 What could be more fun than hitting a pinch-hit grand slam in a big-league game? Only one Red Sox player has done it more than once. Who was he? *(Answer on page 91.)*

31 Which Red Sox batter is tied for the team record for home runs in a single game but stands out because he accomplished it on a very special date? *(Answer on page 91.)*

32 Which Red Sox team scored the most runs in the course of a given season? *(Answer on page 92.)*

33 Striking out is normally one of the worst fates to befall a batter. Which Red Sox team struck out more than any other? *(Answer on page 92.)*

34 Walking isn't hitting, of course, but it gets you on base. Without a doubt, it's better than striking out. When one looks at the list of the top 10 Boston Red Sox batters for drawing the most walks in a given season, what one thing immediately jumps out at you? *(Answer on page 93.)*

35 A team that was 0-for-19 with runners in scoring position, but still won the game? Was there ever such a game for the Red Sox? *(Answer on page 93.)*

36 Since the advent of the DH, of course, Red Sox pitchers normally only come to bat in interleague play at National League ballparks. Starting pitchers tend to get those at-bats. Relief pitchers rarely do. We know that some pitchers from earlier times were good-hitting pitchers—Babe Ruth, Wes Ferrell, Earl Wilson among them. They tended to be starters, not relievers. Which Red Sox reliever has more base hits than any other? *(Answer on page 94.)*

37 From *Day By Day with the Boston Red Sox*: Lots of people know how Ted Williams played in the final doubleheader of the 1941 season and boosted his average to .406. Can you name the Red Sox player who similarly decided to play out the season—and lost a batting title in the process? *(Answer on page 94.)*

38 Ted Williams's .406 batting average in 1941 is the highest ever hit by a Red Sox player. Williams batted left-handed. Who has the highest batting average by a right-handed Red Sox batter? *(Answer on page 94.)*

39 Here are six Red Sox batters. One of them had such a great year that he drove in 25 percent of all the team's game-winning hits that year. Who was he? *(Answer on page 95.)*
Ted Williams
Carl Yastrzemski
Jim Rice
Mike Greenwell
Mike Easler
Mo Vaughn

40 Which pitcher hit two home runs in a game—several times? *(Answer on page 95.)*

41 Is it really true that it took catcher Haywood Sullivan five or six years in the big leagues before he got his first base hit? *(Answer on page 95.)*

42 With 92 extra-base hits in the 1938 season, back in the days of the 154-game schedule, Jimmie Foxx holds the club record for most extra-base hits in a single season. Who holds the Red Sox rookie record for most extra-base hits in his rookie season? *(Answer on page 96.)*

43 On July 4, 2003, switch-hitting Bill Mueller hit home runs from both sides of the plate. Has there ever been a game when two switch-hitters on the same team each hit two home runs? *(Answer on page 96.)*

44 Did any Red Sox player ever hit two inside-the-park home runs in the same game? *(Answer on page 97.)*

45 What Red Sox player had a home run as each of his first three major-league hits? *(Answer on page 97.)*

46 Ancient wisdom? Only once in major-league history have two players aged forty years or older hit home runs in the same game. Can you name the two players? *(Answer on page 97.)*

HITTING ANSWERS

1 First and foremost, perhaps, he drove in 145 runs. That's a lot of RBIs for anyone at any time. Williams also showed his trademark patience at the plate, drawing 107 bases on balls. It's worthy to note that Walt Dropo challenged Ted's RBI record in the 1950 season. He fell one short, driving in 144 runs in his own rookie season. Dropo was named Rookie in the Year in the American League. Twice more (1952 and 1953) Dropo drove in 90-plus runs. Williams drove in more than 100 runs each of his first eight seasons—despite taking off three years during World War II. His high point was 1949, when he drove in 159 runs (in 155 games). Only a broken shoulder in July 1950 (during the All-Star Game) prevented him from doing it again, and even then he drove in 97 runs in 89 games. That's two seasons in a row—1949 and 1950—when he knocked in more than one run per game.

2 Way, way back in 1902, left-fielder Patsy Dougherty hit for a .342 batting average. But eighty years later, in 1982, Wade Boggs hit .349 in his first season. Because Boggs only had 381 plate appearances, he couldn't qualify for the batting title that year. The rule is that a player needs 3.1 plate appearances per team game. Thus, in a

162-game season, that would be 502 plate appearances. Boggs was well shy of that figure.

He won the batting title next year, batting .361 in 1983. So if the question had been phrased to be which team batter won the batting title the first year he was eligible, it would be Boggs. But that wasn't how we phrased the question. As a batter, if you have more than 130 at bats, that's your rookie year. So Boggs was a rookie in 1982 (and, in fact, placed third in ROY balloting).

3 Actually, every one of them except for Jim Rice and Billy Rohr (who was a pitcher). Hobson was perhaps the most unusual one in that it happened so much later than his actual debut. He'd appeared in two road games in 1975, but Butch marked his June 28, 1976, Fenway Park debut with a double off the center-field wall and an inside-the-park home run, helping the Sox win, 12–8, over Baltimore.

Nava's was a grand slam, hit on the first pitch he ever saw. It was an interleague game on June 12, 2010. Nava had never been considered a prospect and was signed out of independent baseball for just one dollar (!) by Red Sox scout Jared Porter. He was playing left field that day. Nava stepped into the batter's box for his first major-league at-bat, facing Joe Blanton of the reigning NL champion Phillies. The bases were loaded. Nava swung at the first pitch he saw and lined it into the Red Sox bullpen. Grand slam. It was only the second time in big-league history that someone hit a grand slam on the very first pitch he saw. When Nava came up for his second time, the bases were loaded again. Now that *really* would have been something . . . but he struck out.

4 It was an inside-the-park home run—hit by perhaps the last man you'd think could leg it around the bases before the ball was thrown home. At Fenway Park on April 25, 1990, the forty-one-year-old player hit a drive off Kirk McCaskill of the Angels. It was a drive to right, and Claudell Washington crashed into the stands, hurting his knee so badly he later had to leave the game. The *Boston Globe*'s Frank Dell'Apa wrote that it was "likely the first homer in which the ball remained in play and the fielder went over the fence."

5 In 1918, when he led the American League with 11 home runs, Babe Ruth hit every one of them on the road. And that isn't even the record for such an imbalanced achievement: in 1926, Goose Goslin of the Washington Senators hit 17 home runs, without even one of them being hit in his home park. He didn't lead the league that year, though. Ruth did.

6 The Silver Slugger Award is one that has only been presented (by Louisville Slugger) since 1980, which therefore excludes a swath of Sox sluggers. There has been no attempt at a "retrospective Silver Slugger Award" yet, so far as we are aware. Wade Boggs won it six times, as did Manny Ramirez. It was a three-way tie until David Ortiz's last season, where he hit .315 and won his seventh award.

7 Right field is easier to answer. We're still waiting. No one ever has hit one out, though Carl Yastrzemski hit one that came very close. It was on June 19, 1977, during a stretch when there were a lot of home runs hammered by Red Sox players. As the *Red Sox Media Guide* describes it: "It reached approximately 460 feet before striking the facing of the right-field roof about 20 feet to the right of where the retired No. 42 now appears. It is the only ball to reach the right-field roof façade."

Hitting a ball out of the park to straightaway center field has been done six times—by Hank Greenberg and Jimmie Foxx (both in 1937), Moose Skowron (twenty years later, in 1957), Carl Yastrzemski (1970), Bobby Mitchell (1973), and Jim Rice (1975). As part of the renovations started after the 1975 World Series, which resulted in padding being placed on the outfield walls, a tall barrier perhaps six to ten feet tall was placed atop the brick wall behind the seats in the center-field bleachers. That remained in place until the 2002 season. Even though it's been removed, no one has yet hit one all the way out since Rice's 1975 blast.

There were indeed a lot of home runs hit at that point in 1977. In fact, in the three-game series when Yaz nearly hit one out, the Sox out-homered the Yankees, 16–0. Red Sox manager Don Zimmer said, "Guys were gettin' blisters shakin' hands."

8 On June 4, 1946, Ted Williams hit a home run to the 37th row of the right-field bleachers. The spot where the ball landed was on the head of construction engineer Joseph A. Boucher, who claimed to have been dozing off on the warm spring afternoon when the ball hit off his head, puncturing a hole in his straw hat. "They say it bounced a dozen rows higher," Boucher told Harold Kaese of the *Boston Globe*. The site is today marked by a lone red seat in the sea of green seats that today comprises the right-field and center-field bleachers. There was no seat there at the time; bleacherites didn't get individual seats until after the 1977 season. Before that, everyone sat on thick wooden planks.

On June 23, 2001, Manny Ramirez hit a ball that was still rising when it hit the left-most light tower above the Green Monster. The Red Sox announced that Manny Ramirez's massive drive had an estimated probable distance of 501 feet, conveniently one foot shorter than Ted's home run.

9 We can answer the "natural cycle" first—a Sox batter has only accomplished that twice (making it historically as rare as an unassisted triple play) and neither time was at Fenway Park: Bob Watson did it most recently in a game at Baltimore on September 15, 1979. The only other one for the Red Sox was hit by Leon Culberson on July 3, 1943, in Cleveland.

Now, as to hitting for the cycle without worrying about the sequence, five times opponents have done this to the Red Sox at Fenway (and another time in a Red Sox home game played at Braves Field). The Red Sox have done it 10 times; the only Red Sox player who's done it twice is Bobby Doerr, and both times were at Fenway: on May 17, 1944, and on May 13, 1947. Joe Cronin did it twice in games involving the Red Sox, once as a member of the Red Sox and once before joining the Red Sox as a member of the Washington Senators.

Red Sox owner Tom Yawkey with Joe Cronin.

10 Johnny Damon. On June 27, 2003. He hit a single, a double, and a triple—all in the first inning of the game against the Florida Marlins. In the process, he tied the major-league record for hits in an inning, sharing it with Boston's Gene Stephens (June 18, 1953). By the time he'd had those three hits, everyone was hoping he'd come up again and homer.

The fact that Damon got three at-bats in one inning made it clear this was a very big inning. The first seven Sox batters collected hits off starter Carl Pavano and reliever Michael Tejera. Then there was a walk, followed by a single, a triple, and a single. At this point, Marlins manager Jack McKeon called on his third pitcher of the game. Ten men had come to bat and there were no outs, and Damon already had his single and his triple and had scored twice.

Allen Levrault took over pitching. He got Nomar Garciaparra to hit a foul popup behind home plate. One out. There followed a single, a walk, a sacrifice fly (out #2, but with another run crossing the plate), and then a walk, a double, a walk, and Johnny Damon was up for a third time. He singled, driving in the 14th run of the inning. It's conceivable the Sox could have kept the inning going, and going, but Bill Mueller got a little too aggressive, trying to score the 15th run on Damon's single, and he was thrown out at home plate.

By the time the game was over, the Red Sox scored 25 runs—without even having to bat in the bottom of the ninth. Can you guess which team won the game? Yes, Boston Red Sox 25, Florida Marlins 8.

11 "I would have stopped at first base." That's just how rare a feat a cycle is.

12 Yes, Brock Holt—the Brockstar—on June 16, 2015, against the visiting Atlanta Braves. It was nearly twenty years between Red Sox cycles. An interesting side note: Bobby Doerr is the only Red Sox player to hit for the cycle twice, once on May 17, 1944, and again on May 13, 1947, both times at Fenway.

13 Blake Swihart, in the 10th inning of a game, no less. It was on August 28, 2015, in the top of the 10th at Citi Field against the New York Mets. Carlos Torres was pitching, and Swihart was the first batter up in the inning. Fortunately, the Sox added two more runs later in the 10th, because the Mets got one run back in the bottom of the inning. But they only got one back.

14 It was Bill Mueller. The switch-hitting Mueller hit for a .326 batting average in 2003. He won it by a hair, beating out teammate Manny Ramirez, .326 to .325. It was a race that went down to the final day. Derek Jeter was a close third, with a .324 average. Mueller was 1-for-4 in his last two games. Ramirez didn't play. Jeter went 0-for-3, dropping him from .326 to .324. Mueller had been hitting .327 and would have batted earlier in the game had Jeter gotten a hit. He didn't, and Mueller had an "at-bat to spare." So when Jeter was replaced in his game, manager Grady Little put in Mueller to pinch-hit. He made an out and dropped from .327 to .326. But Mueller still had the title.

15 Jimmie Foxx. In 1938, "The Beast" drove in 175 runs. Second on the all-time Red Sox list was the Williams/Stephens combo in 1949—both of them had 159 RBIs. Add 159 + 159, and the two together drove in 318 runs.

Jimmie Foxx chatting with a Fenway ticket seller.

David Ortiz comes next, with his 148 in 2005. The highest total that did not result in winning the RBI crown was the 144 that Manny Ramirez drove in that very same year, 2005—because Ortiz drove in four more runs. In the 1938 season, Foxx drove in more than 100 runs at Fenway Park alone! He had 104 home RBIs and 71 on the road.

16 The first two never accomplished that. Neither Foxx nor Williams drove in 10 runs in a game. The others did. Rudy York was the first; he did it on July 27, 1946. Norm Zauchin did it next, on May 27, 1955. Fred Lynn did so on June 18, 1975, and Nomar Garciaparra did it on May 10, 1999.

17 Tuffy Rhodes. In six seasons in the major leagues, Rhodes hit 13 homers. His last year in the majors was with

the Red Sox (1995), and he hit zero home runs that year. In 2001, playing for Osaka's Kintetsu Buffaloes, he hit 55 homers, tying Sadaharu Oh's record. From that point on in the season, he never got a single pitch that would enable him to surpass Oh. Two years later, in 2003, he hit 51 homers for the Buffaloes.

18 In 1978, Jim Ed Rice recorded a total of 406 total bases. He hit a major league–leading 46 homers, which gave him 184 total bases. He hit a major league–leading 15 triples, which gave him another 45 bases. And he doubled 25 times. That adds 50 more. And he singled 127 times. Rice's 213 base hits led both leagues. Rice was the league MVP. He's the last batter in the American League who has hit for a total of 400 or more bases. Oddly, it's been done seven times in the National League since, four times in the year 2001.

19 We figured we had to slip in a few easier questions here. With a lifetime on-base percentage of .482, Ted Williams ranks higher than anyone else who ever played the game. Someone had to come first, of course, but consider the number. That means that almost half the time Ted Williams came to bat, he got on base—48.2 percent of the time—in a career that spanned parts of four decades (1939 through 1960), a career that was interrupted twice by Williams leaving baseball for military service, in World War II and the Korean War. His 1941 season saw him with a .553 on-base percentage. The top nine Red Sox season stats for OBP all belong to Ted Williams. Ranking 10th on the list is Wade

Boggs, who had an on-base percentage of .476 in the 1988 season.

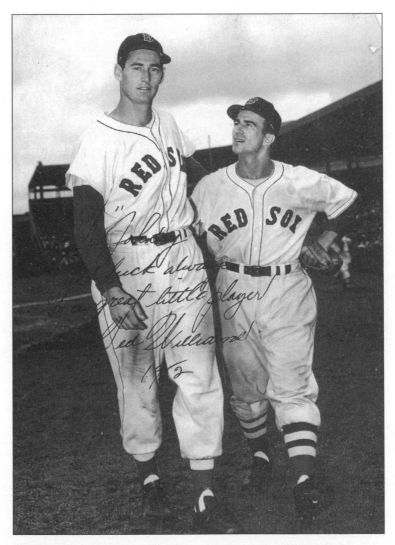

Photograph signed by Ted Williams and presented to Johnny Pesky.

20 Neither Ted nor Yaz ever reached 200. Ted Williams's highest total was 194 (1949), and Yaz's was 191 (1962). Nomar hit safely 209 times in 1997. Jim Rice hit 200 or more hits four times—1977, 1978, 1979, and 1986. Boggs did it seven years in a row, from 1983 through 1987. Pesky? He did it his first three seasons, but not after that.

21 We're not trying to make Jim Rice feel bad. After all, he's a Hall of Famer! But there was one downside. From 1982 through 1985, Rice led the league in grounding into double plays. Ernie Lombardi led his league four times in GIDP, but never more than twice in succession. The most he hit into was 30 in 1938—the same year he was National League MVP.

Rice's 36 GIDP in 1984 is the major-league record. (Rice also had 122 RBIs that very same year.)

22 He's probably not someone you would have guessed. It is Jackie Bradley Jr. On August 15, 2015, he hit two home runs and four doubles (driving in seven runs) as the Red Sox slaughtered Seattle by a score of 22–10.

23 Jimmie Foxx had five. Manny Ramirez had six. Ted Williams had eight. And David Ortiz had ten: 2003, 2004, 2005, 2006, 2007, 2010, 2013, 2014, 2015, and 2016.

24 The most exhaustive study of Ted Williams's homer-hitting exploits (even including high school, minor-league, and All-Star Game home runs) is *521: The Story of Ted Williams' Home Runs* (Rounder Books, 2013). The correct answer is 96, and every one of them is detailed in the book (which happens to have been written by me).

25 Yes. Who, you ask? Ted Williams. In 1941, he homered 37 times but only whiffed 27 times. In 1950, he hit 28 homers and struck out 21 times—all before breaking his elbow in the All-Star Game and missing half the season. In 1955, he struck out 24 times and hit 28 homers. After he returned from flying combat missions for the Marines in the Korean War, Williams played a partial season in 1953, homering 13 times but only striking out 10 times. In all, then, he did so a remarkable four times.

In case you were wondering, when Babe Ruth hit 60 home runs for the Yankees in 1927, he also struck out more than anyone in both leagues (89). Roger Maris was closer; in 1961 he homered 61 times and struck out 67 times. When Barry Bonds homered 73 times for the Giants in 2001, he struck out 93 times. During the Sosa-McGwire battle year of 1998, both struck out more than twice as many times as they homered: Sosa hit 66 homers but struck out 171 times, while McGwire hit 70 homers and struck out 155 times.

26 Ted Williams reached base 16 times in a row from September 17 through September 23, 1957—and the first three times were in pinch-hitting roles:
Sept. 17 vs. KC: pinch-hit home run
Sept. 18 vs. KC: pinch-hit walk
Sept. 20 at NY: pinch-hit home run
Sept. 21 at NY: home run, three walks

Sept. 22 at NY: home run, single, two walks
Sept. 23 at NY: single, three walks, hit by pitch

27 You probably guessed correctly. Ted Williams. From July 1, 1949, to September 27, 1949 (in other words, more than half the season), Williams reached base safely in every game he played, for a Consecutive Games on Base Safely (CGOBS) streak of 84 games in a row. As it happens, in all of 1949, Ted only failed to reach base five times: June 3, 7, 26, 30, and September 28.

Think about this—in more than a decade of play (even including three years in military service), if one is willing to exclude a pinch-hit appearance in 1941 and another in 1948, Williams never had back-to-back games of not getting on base safely, from July 14, 1940, through September 26, 1950.

28 Jim Landis, on August 24, 1967. He hit 93 home runs in the majors but was 1-for-7 in his brief time with the Red Sox. It was a solo home run hit off Washington's Darold Knowles in the bottom of the eighth inning at Fenway Park. It provided an extra insurance run in a 7–5 Red Sox victory.

29 Babe Ruth. In fact, Ruth only hit a total of nine home runs from 1914 through 1917 (we acknowledge that he hit zero home runs his first season, but he only appeared in five games.) In 1918, he homered 11 times, but none were grand slams. One was a three-run homer. And, as you may recall from an earlier question, every home run he hit was hit on the road. Finally, in 1919, Ruth hit four grand slams (among his 29 homers). All the slams were hit in road games.

30 It was Vic Wertz. The first time was August 14, 1959, at Yankee Stadium, batting against Ryne Duren in the top of the eighth. The score had been 6–2, Yankees. After Wertz trotted around the bases, it was 6–6. The next August he faced Don Newcombe at Fenway Park, on the 25th of the month. The Sox had just scored a run in the bottom of the third to tie the game with the Indians at 4–4. The bases were loaded, and Wertz was asked to hit for Bill Monbouquette. With one swing of the bat, Wertz doubled the score and made it 8–4, Red Sox.

31 The date was July 23, 2002. It was Nomar Garciaparra's 29th birthday. He hit two homers in one inning, the third. They helped build a 10-run inning. The next

Nomar Garciaparra and Johnny Pesky.

inning, he hit another one. Nomar, however, is not the only Sox player to hit three homers in one game. The most recent (at press time) is Mookie Betts, on May 31, 2016.

32 It was the 1950 team, the only Red Sox team to ever score over 1,000 runs. The Sox scored 1,027 runs that year (hitting for a team average of .302), despite it being a 154-game season compared to today's 162-game schedule. That's an average of 6.67 runs per game. The equivalent for a 162-game season would be 1,080 run.

33 It had been the 2004 World Champion Red Sox, who struck out 1,189 times. But since that very good year, the Sox set new highs (lows?) three years in a row: 2012 (1,197 strikeouts), 2013 (1,308 strikeouts), and 2014 (1,337 strikeouts). It may be of interest to note that two of the top four years for high-K totals are World Champion years—2004 and 2013. In 2007, the Sox "only" whiffed 1,042 times. It may also be of interest that the 1903 Boston Americans only struck out 559 times. In 1912, the champs struck out 586 times. The three other championship years were 1915 (476), 1916 (482), and 1918 (324). Looking again at the 2014 season, Xander Bogaerts struck out 138 times, Mike Napoli struck out 133 times, and Jackie Bradley Jr. struck out 121 times. The three combined for 392 Ks, 68 more than the entire 1918 team. (It may be noted, however, that the 1918 team only played 126 games, in that wartime-truncated season.) The 1915 team was probably the best team at not striking out.

34 They're almost all named Ted Williams. In fact, if you look at the top seven of them, every one of them is named Ted Williams.

162: Ted Williams, 1947
162: Ted Williams, 1949
156: Ted Williams, 1946
147: Ted Williams, 1941
145: Ted Williams, 1942
144: Ted Williams, 1951
136: Ted Williams, 1954
128: Carl Yastrzemski, 1970
126: Ted Williams, 1948
125: Wade Boggs, 1988

Of the ten, the only one who didn't lead the league in walks during the year in question was Carl Yastrzemski.

In a sense, that Ted Williams holds eight of the top 10 slots might not seem so surprising when you know that Mr. Williams leads the major leagues all-time in walks percentage. Of all the times he came to the plate, he was walked 20.65 percent of the time, more than any other player in baseball history.

35 In the April 24, 2004, game against the New York Yankees, a Boston Red Sox batter came to the plate 19 times with a runner in scoring position and never once in the game did any one of those batters get a hit. Nonetheless, they won the game, 3–2, in 12 innings. Fortunately (for Red Sox fans), there were three sacrifice flies.

36 The Monster—Dick Radatz with 16 base hits to his credit. Radatz was often a "long reliever," pitching multiple innings at a time. In his time with the Red Sox, Radatz pitched 557 1/3 innings in 286 games, thus averaging almost two innings (1.945) per outing. It's not that he was a great batter; his batting average with Boston was a lowly .127. He got one home run among those 16 hits, but it was a game-winner. Top of the 11th inning at Kansas City's Municipal Stadium, the solo home run off Jesse Hickman broke a 3–3 tie. It was a game in which Radatz pitched three innings—the ninth, 10th, and 11th—and won the game.

37 This did happen, and it was in 1970. On September 30, Carl Yastrzemski lost his chance at another batting title. After his second at-bat in the game, Yaz was at .3297872. "I legged out an infield single. I twisted my ankle and should have came [sic] out of the ballgame. It's your back leg, where all the weight is. But I stayed in." He stayed in and made two more outs, reducing his average to .3286219. Alex Johnson of the Angels went 2-for-3 and ended his day with an average of .32899. Had Yaz come out of a game that meant nothing in the standings . . .

38 Nomar Garciaparra does—his .372 batting average in the year 2000 stands as the highest by a right-handed hitter. It's worth noting that second-highest overall was Ted Williams' .388 in 1957, the year he turned thirty-nine years old. And the third-highest was Tris Speaker in 1912, when he hit .383. Speaker was also left-handed.

39 He played left field and wore #39. In 1988, Mike Greenwell led the team both in home runs (22) and RBIs (119). His third-inning single in the September 29 contest drove in that game's winning hit. It was his 23rd game-winning hit in 1988. "Gator" holds the American League record for game-winning hits in a season. That year's Red Sox team won 89 games, and Greenwell recorded the game-winning hit in more than 25 percent of them.

40 On August 22, 1934, in Boston, pitcher Wes Ferrell tied the game against the White Sox at 2–2 with a home run in the bottom of the eighth inning. When he came up to bat the next time, it was the bottom of the 10th. He hit another out of the park. He hit both homers off Les Tietje. The *Chicago Tribune* noted: "Both sailed over the left center field wall, the final one being such a long drive that the Chicago outfielders were on their way off the field before it disappeared from view." It was the second time in 1934 that Ferrell hit two homers in a game; he did it six times in his career.

41 In a sense. Look it up. Sullivan later became president of the Red Sox and a part-owner of the team. His major-league debut with the Red Sox was in 1955. He had six at-bats but did not make a hit. Never leaving the Red Sox system, he appeared in big-league games in 1957 and 1959 without a base hit. Finally, in his second game in 1960, he singled. So that's from 1955 into 1960 . . .

42 It actually was set the very next year, 1939—also in the days of the 154-game schedule. The rookie was Ted Williams, with 86 extra-base hits. The Kid had 31 homers, 44 doubles, and 11 triples. He hit 14 triples in 1940, but never again more than nine.

43 Yes, there has. That very same game. Switch-hitter Jason Varitek also hit two homers in the game. Spoiling much of the fun, though, Varitek hit both of his batting from the same side of the plate.

Jason Varitek crosses home plate after a home run.

44 Of course there was. Otherwise, we wouldn't have asked the question! In fact, it happened four times: Hobe Ferris (May 4, 1903), Heinie Wagner (August 22, 1907), Larry Gardner (July 2, 1912), and Hal Janvrin (October 4, 1913). Wagner's were the first two home runs he ever hit in the majors. In all of 1912, Gardner only hit one other home run.

45 Mike Greenwell, in 1985. His homers on September 25, September 26, and October 1 were his first three big-league hits.

46 Leading off the second inning, Alex Rodriguez (40) of the New York Yankees hit a solo home run in the April 29, 2016, game at Fenway Park, giving New York a 1–0 lead. In the bottom of the eighth inning, with the score tied, 2–2, David Ortiz (40) homered with a man aboard, off ace reliever Dellin Betances, with what proved to be the game-winning hit for the Red Sox.

6

FIELDING

How about some fun facts about fielding?

1 Who is the Red Sox player who holds the longest streak of consecutive games played without committing an error? *(Answer on page 101.)*

2 Which of these three Red Sox fielders recorded assists at a faster rate? *(Answer on page 102.)*
   A. Ted Williams
   B. Carl Yastrzemski
   C. Dwight Evans

3 There was one Red Sox player who fielded at least one ball but goes down in history with a lifetime fielding percentage of .000. Can you name him? *(Answer on page 102.)*

4 There was one Red Sox infielder—and only one—who played an entire season (at least 100 games) without committing even one error. Who was it? *(Answer on page 103.)*

5 Which Sox player won the most Gold Gloves, once you exclude the outfielders Carl Yastrzemski (7), Fred Lynn (4), and Dwight Evans (8)? *(Answer on page 104.)*

6 First baseman Dick Stuart was nicknamed "Dr. Strange-glove." He wasn't considered the best fielder in the game, or on the Red Sox. In 1963, he led the American League in RBIs, with 118. And he led the league in total bases, with 319. What other league-leading marks did he hold that year? *(Answer on page 105.)*

7 What Red Sox team is the best-fielding Red Sox team in franchise history? *(Answer on page 105.)*

8 If you're talking Tommy Hottovy, you're talking a little obscure (sorry, Tommy). The pitcher debuted for the Red Sox on June 3, 2011. He only threw four innings for the Red Sox. Double credit if you can describe the obscure fact that characterized his first three outings. We'll even give you a hint to help out: David DeJesus. *(Answer on page 105.)*

9 Can you name the Red Sox player—a pitcher—who converted the last fielding chance in his major-league career into a triple play? *(Answer on page 105.)*

FIELDING ANSWERS

1 Yooooooouk! That translates to Kevin Youkilis, who played in 238 consecutive games without making an error. Youk's streak stretched from July 5, 2006, to June 6, 2008—almost two years!

Youk!

2 With 140 outfield assists in 2,292 games, Ted Williams recorded an outfield assist every 16.37 games. Gold Glover Dwight Evans quickly earned the reputation that you didn't run on his arm, so while he played in 2,505 Red Sox games, he only recorded 151 outfield assists (once every 16.96 games). Yaz had 195 outfield assists, but he played a lot of first base and DH. He was in fewer games (2,076) as an outfielder, giving him one assist every 10.65 games.

3 You win if you joined the chorus of those who cried out, "Yes! Ralph Pond!" He played center field in just one game, in Chicago on June 8, 1910. Pond was an outfielder and had just one chance—which he muffed. He did better at the plate, singling once in four at-bats. The *Boston Herald* wrote that he "looked the part of a ballplayer at bat." He goes down in history with a .250 batting average. Pond even has a stolen base to his credit. But his lifetime fielding percentage is indeed .000. He also misjudged two others, both of which went for base hits. He was taken out of the game, and Charley "Sea Lion" Hall—a pitcher—replaced Pond in center for defensive purposes in the eighth inning. Pond was, in the words of the *Boston Post*, "given the G.B" (the grand bounce). The White Sox beat the Red Sox, 5–4, but it took them 11 innings to do so.

The newspapers covering the game weren't impressed. "Weird Fielding Lost Game for Red Sox," headlined the *Post*. Commenting on Pond's performance that day, the *Boston Globe* presciently noted: "Just at the present the sturdy collegian won't do, for he loomed up sadly deficient in the fine points of middle fielding." He wasn't alone in the miscue department; the Sox made seven errors that day. The *Chicago Tribune* was a little rougher on him. "A bum finger kept [Tris] Speaker out of the game and a recruit named Pond started to fill his shoes. The youngster may be a Pond in Maine but he was hardly a puddle in center field. In fact, he did not cover much more ground on fly balls than a good sized raindrop. After he had misjudged two which went for hits, pitcher Hall was sent out there in the eighth."

4 Kevin Youkilis, in 2007. And it wasn't as though he didn't have that many chances. Youk recorded 990 putouts and earned 90 assists—a full 1,080 chances without even one error. There were some outfielders who had error-free seasons:

Ken Harrelson, 1968: 249 chances (he did commit three errors at first base that year)

Carl Yastrzemski, 1977: 303 chances (he also handled 63 error-free chances at first base)

Jacoby Ellsbury, 2008: 336 chances

Jason Bay, 2009: 325 chances

Jacoby Ellsbury, 2011: 394 chances

There were two catchers:

Pete Daley, 1957: 309 chances

Rick Cerone, 1988: 499 chances

And four pitchers (minimum, 60 chances):

Jack Russell, 1929: 84 chances
Mel Parnell, 1949: 61 chances
Bill Monbouquette, 1963: 68 chances
Derek Lowe, 2003: 65 chances

Somehow it seems there should be more pitchers, but that's the way it is.

5 Dustin Pedroia has four of them, George Scott had three, and Frank Malzone had three.

Always the first on the bench, Dustin Pedroia.

6 In 1963, he also led the league in errors (with 29) and in GIDP with 24, tied with teammate Frank Malzone.

7 The year was 2006. The Red Sox overall had a team fielding percentage of .98910. The 2006 team holds the team record for the fewest errors—66 errors in a 162-game season. They also pulled off a record 108 errorless games during the course of the season.

8 In his debut, Hottovy faced one batter and got Oakland's David DeJesus to ground out. On June 4, Hottovy faced one batter—DeJesus—and got him to ground out. And on June 5, Hottovy appeared in his third major-league game, retiring one batter (DeJesus) and inducing a ground out. He did walk a guy. His first big-league appearances saw him retire the same batter three times, each time with the same result.

9 It was a pitcher, Pete Smith, on September 28, 1963. The Angels had runners on first and second with nobody out, and a 3–2 lead. Looking for an insurance run, Felix Torres bunted to advance both runners but popped the ball up to the mound. Smith ran forward, but shortstop Eddie Bressoud yelled at Smith to let the ball drop. Alertly, he did and then kicked off a 1-5-6-4 triple play.

7

POSTSEASON PLAY

1 Getting into the postseason requires winning the pennant. These days, that's a multi-step process involving winning the Division Series and the League Championship Series, and potentially a game to win the wild card before either of those two stages. Looking at David Ortiz's heroics in the 2004 ALCS, where he hit walkoff hits to win back-to-back elimination games against the New York Yankees, one would be hard-pressed to argue that anyone did more to win a pennant. But there's at least one other candidate who should come to the mind of most Red Sox fans. Who is he, and what did he do at crunch time? *(Answer on page 113.)*

2 Which pitchers for the franchise won three World Series games, all in the same year? *(Answer on page 113.)*

3 Which Red Sox pitcher has won three deciding games in postseason play? We're not talking just three games, like in that last question (though that is plenty impressive), but three deciding games? *(Answer on page 113.)*

4 Being 1–0 in the World Series makes a pitcher undefeated. But one game could be a fluke. What pitcher has the best postseason record of any pitcher in baseball history who has at least 10 decisions to his name? *(Answer on page 115.)*

A. Babe Ruth

B. Boo Ferriss

C. Pedro Martinez

D. Curt Schilling

E. Smoky Joe Wood

5 Why was it that when the 1914 World Series was played at Fenway Park, the Red Sox never took the field at any point during any of the games? *(Answer on page 115.)*

6 Why was it that the team once won the American League pennant but went home and didn't play the World Series? *(Answer on page 116.)*

7 The Red Sox famously came back from being down three games to none in the 2004 American League Championship Series and taking four games in a row from the Yankees, and then sweeping St. Louis in the World Series—for eight consecutive wins. The Red Sox then lost their next postseason game, to the White Sox in 2005. Not that we want to wallow in defeat, but what is the longest run of postseason losses the Red Sox have ever borne? *(Answer on page 117.)*

8 There is one particular team that the Red Sox beat time after time in the postseason. The Sox just had this team's number. What was the team and how many postseason games in a row did the Red Sox beat them? *(Answer on page 117.)*

9 Which Red Sox batter had the highest batting average in the 2004 World Series? *(Answer on page 119.)*

A. David Ortiz

B. Manny Ramirez

C. Bill Mueller

D. Johnny Damon

E. Mark Bellhorn

10 In what year did the Red Sox play the World Series, start to finish, in the month of September? *(Answer on page 119.)*

11 What is the unlikely, but somewhat wonderful, thing about the four times the Red Sox lost the World Series? *(Answer on page 119.)*

12 Babe Ruth played in three World Series for the Red Sox— 1915, 1916, and 1918. The Red Sox won all three of those World Series. How many total homers did Ruth hit, and how many runs did he drive in? *(Answer on page 119.)*

13 How about Ted Williams? When he played in the 1946 World Series, how did he do? *(Answer on page 120.)*

14 Who was the offensive star for the Red Sox in the 1946 World Series? *(Answer on page 122.)*

15 Can you name the World Series MVPs in the three twenty-first century world championships the Red Sox have won? That would be 2004, 2007, and 2013. Easy, right? Maybe not. *(Answer on page 122.)*

16 What's the case that can be made for a .250 hitter being the MVP of one of Boston's World Championships? (No, we are not talking about a pitcher.) *(Answer on page 123.)*

17 Why did Boston have to play eight games in the 1903 World Series and again in the 1912 World Series? *(Answer on page 123.)*

18 In the 1915 World Series, the Red Sox only scored 12 runs all Series long, but still won—even though the Series ran five games. Was there ever a World Series which the Sox won with fewer runs? *(Answer on page 123.)*

19 A 20-game winner, but after two innings, he was yanked from his early World Series start and never allowed to pitch again in the Series. Who was he? *(Answer on page 124.)*

20 There's nothing like a grand slam to win a pennant. In 2013, in Game Six at Fenway Park, the Detroit Tigers held a thin 2–1 lead as the Red Sox came to bat in the bottom of the seventh inning. A double, a walk, and an error loaded the bases. There was one out. What Boston batter banged the ball out for a grand slam? *(Answer on page 125.)*

21 Who's the only member of the Red Sox to have played for four world champion Red Sox teams? *(Answer on page 125.)*

POSTSEASON PLAY ANSWERS

1 We're thinking of Carl Yastrzemski. In 1967, as four teams battled for the pennant, three of them right down to the last hours of the last day of the regular season. Over the final 12 games of the season, Yaz had 23 hits in 44 at-bats, driving in 16 runs and scoring 14. He had 10 hits in his last 13 at-bats, and when it came to the last two games with the Twins, with the Sox needing to win both games to help avert a tie for the pennant, Yaz went 7-for-8 and drove in six runs.

When it came to the World Series, he didn't let up, either, batting .400 with three homers and five runs batted in.

2 Bill Dinneen pitched for the Boston Americans in the 1903 World Series, winning Game Two, Game Six, and Game Eight (in a best-of-nine series); and Smoky Joe Wood pitched for the Red Sox in 1912. Smoky Joe won Games One, Four, and Eight. Game Two was called a tie at 6–6 after 11 innings on account of darkness. In 1903, Dinneen also lost a game, so he had decisions in half of his team's games, going 3–1.

3 Derek Lowe—all in the same year! It was 2004. Lowe came on in relief in Game Three of the American League

Division Series and pitched the top of the 10th inning of a 6–6 game against the Angels. That's all he needed to get the win, when David Ortiz hit a two-run homer in the bottom of the 10th.

The first trophy in eighty-six years.

In the AL Championship Series against New York, he started Game Four but was long gone when that game was resolved (by another Ortiz two-run walk-off home run) in the bottom of the 12th. He did, however, start Game Seven as well, at Yankee Stadium, and left after six innings with an 8–1 lead. The Sox bullpen held that lead.

Lowe started Game Four of the World Series, in St. Louis, with the Red Sox having already won the first three games. This time he pitched shutout ball for seven innings (just three hits and one walk), and the three innings the Sox had scored early on held up. That makes three Ws, credited with the win in the ALDS, ALCS, and the World Series. Not too shabby.

4 The answer is Curt Schilling, who was 11–2 in the post-season. For the Philadelphia Phillies, he was 1–1. For the Arizona Diamondbacks, he was 4–0, and for the Sox he was 6–1.

5 Most of them had gone home. The Red Sox didn't win the pennant. They finished in second place, 8.5 games behind the Philadelphia Athletics. But the Boston Braves (the "Miracle Braves") won the National League pennant. Since Fenway Park was a larger facility and could accommodate more paying customers, arrangements were made to have the Braves play their home games at Fenway. They swept the Series from the Athletics in four games, with Games Three and Four played to capacity crowds at Fenway.

6 They were willing to, but the National League pennant winners, the New York Giants, refused to play them. This was in 1904. The American League had just begun in 1901 and many of the members on the 1901 Boston Americans were recruits from the National League, enticed to quit the NL and come over to the "Junior Circuit." The NL and its teams felt aggrieved, and there were many feelings of "war" between the two leagues. In 1903, there was an agreement between the Pittsburg Pirates and the Boston Americans—winners in their respective leagues—to play each other in a best-of-nine "World's Series." (At the time Pittsburg was spelled without the "h.") They did, and the series went eight games, followed closely by baseball fans across the country. It was a great success, and in negotiations between the two leagues before the 1904 season began, there was agreement for the two league champions to play each other after the regular season was done.

The New York Giants clinched the NL race very early. Despite the overwhelming national sentiment for a series between the two pennant winners, manager John McGraw and owner John T. Brush of the Giants refused to take part, saying in so many words that they were proud to have become champions and weren't going to lower themselves to playing a "minor league" like the American League. (They had a number of players who were hurt, and it could also well have been that they were afraid Boston would beat them.) Even the New York newspapers condemned the Giants' stance (as it happens, the Boston Americans had fought the New York Highlanders—now the Yankees—down to the final day of the season to win the pennant). The Giants players wanted to engage Boston, as it would have made them all quite a lot of extra money. There were reportedly three players whom Brush paid to leave the team even before the end of the season, giving them as much money as they likely would have made in a World Series so they would leave town and *not* play.

The sentiment was so strong that, while the Series was not played, the Giants more or less ate crow before the end of October, and as of 1905, the World Series became an annual event.

Not having been dethroned, the Boston Americans remained champions of the world for yet another year, until the 1905 World Series was concluded.

7 It was an extraordinary (and extraordinarily discouraging) run of 13 losses in a row. The first two were Games Six and Seven of the 1986 World Series. They were then swept four games in a row in the 1988 ALCS, four games in a row by Oakland in the 1990 ALCS, and three more in the 1995 ALDS at the hands of the Cleveland Indians. Finally, in 1998, they won the first game of the ALDS, again versus the Indians, but then lost the next three.

8 It was the Angels, no matter which Angels they were. They were the California Angels in 1986, when they took a three-games-to-one lead in the American League Championship Series. But then came Game Five. The Angels had a 5–2 lead after eight innings. Three more outs, and the Angels were going to the World Series. Don Baylor hit a two-run homer off Mike Witt. Gary Lucas came in to pitch to Rich Gedman, and he did—but he hit him. Out with Lucas, in with Donnie Moore—who gave up a two-run homer to Dave Henderson. The Sox took a 6–5 lead. The Angels tied it with one in the bottom of the ninth, but with the bases loaded and nobody out in the top of the 12th, and Moore still pitching, Hendu came up again and hit a sacrifice fly. One run, but enough to win the game. The Red Sox then won Games Six and Seven.

In 2004, they were the Anaheim Angels, up against the Red Sox in that year's Division Series. The Sox swept the Angels in three games, but it wasn't without a fight. After six innings in Game Three, facing elimination and being down 6–1 heading into the seventh, the Angels got one run, and then Vladimir Guerrero hit a grand slam to tie it. It went into extra innings, but, in the bottom of the 10th, David Ortiz hit a walk-off home run to advance the Sox to the next stage (while recording their sixth win in a row against the Angels).

Three years later, the two teams faced each other again in the ALDS. This time, the team had renamed itself again as the Los Angeles Angels of Anaheim. Once again, the Sox swept the series in three. That made nine wins in a row.

The very next year, 2008, it was another matchup, and the Sox won the first two games, in Anaheim, but then came back home looking to win #12 in succession and were stymied. It took them 12 innings, but the Angels took the game, 5–4. Boston won the next day and went on to the ALCS. Anaheim went home, but after 11 losses in a row, they might have felt something like a moral victory. Maybe. (They had won the World Series in 2002 but hadn't had to go through the Red Sox to get there.)

9 It was Bill Mueller, who hit for a .429 batting average. Manny hit .412, Ortiz batted .308, Mark Bellhorn hit .300, and Johnny Damon hit .286. Now, in terms of RBIs, just to add a little bit here, Bellhorn drove in four, as did David Ortiz and Manny Ramirez. Damon and Mueller each drove in two—but we also wish to mention that both Orlando Cabrera and Trot Nixon drove in three and Jason Varitek drove in two.

10 Because of the First World War, the 1918 season was truncated (the Red Sox played 126 games in the regular season), and the World Series (Red Sox vs. Cubs) was played start to finish in September. The Series ran six games, but Game Six was on September 11, and thus the World Series was over and done with before hitting mid-September.

11 Each time they lost, they went down fighting. Not only were they never swept, they took each World Series to the full seven games. Unfortunately, they did this for four World Series appearances in succession: 1946, 1967, 1975, and 1986. There are those who were born after 1918 and died before 2004 who never lived to see the Red Sox as world champions.

12 He didn't hit any home runs. In fact, even though he took part in all three Series, he only got 11 at-bats in all three Series combined. He drove in one run in 1916 and two runs in 1918. But he won three games as a pitcher, one in 1916 and two in 1918. He's thus 3–0 in World Series pitching for the Red Sox, with an overall earned run average of 0.87.

In 1915, he wasn't asked to pitch, and he was only given one at-bat (he grounded out to first base, unassisted) in the ninth inning of Game One. He was kind of in the doghouse that October, and manager Bill Carrigan was showing him that the team didn't really need him to win.

The three RBIs he got were important ones. The first came in Game Two of the 1916 World Series against Brooklyn. He drove in one run in the bottom of the third inning, with a groundout, tying the game at 1–1. That was the final score, too—neither a win nor a loss, the game was called a tie after 14 innings. Ruth pitched all 14, but he wouldn't have been pitching after nine if he hadn't driven in that one run. His other two RBIs came in Game Four of the 1918 World Series against the Cubs. In the bottom of the fourth inning of a scoreless game, Ruth tripled to deep right-center, driving in George Whiteman and Stuffy McInnis. Working the mound, he allowed two runs through eight innings. In the bottom of the eighth, a single, passed ball, and error gave the Red Sox the one run they needed for a 3–2 win, giving them a three-games-to-one lead in the Series.

13   He didn't do that well. The 1946 Red Sox clinched the American League pennant early and then had to wait

while two National League teams held a playoff series for the pennant. While they were killing time, the Sox were able to bring together a team of American League

Mr. Red Sox, Johnny Pesky.

all-stars (including Joe DiMaggio) to play them at Fenway Park and give them some competition. Pitcher Mickey Haefner of the Washington Senators hit Williams on the right elbow in the fifth inning. It immediately raised a knot the Associated Press said was "about the size of an egg." There was some question whether he would even be able to play in the World Series. He did, but he only hit for a .200 batting average and had a grand total of one RBI, with a first-inning single driving in Johnny Pesky in Game Five. (He'd hit .342 in the regular season and driven in 123 runs.) Stan Musial, with the Cardinals in the same Series, hit .222 but drove in four runs.

14 As we just saw, it wasn't Ted Williams. It was, pretty undeniably, Rudy York. He drove in five runs. Dom DiMaggio and Bobby Doerr each drove in three and Pinky Higgins drove in two. No one else drove in more than one. And York's 10th-inning home run in Game One was the game-winning hit in that game. His three-run homer in the first inning of Game Three was the game winner there, too—a game Boston won, 4–0, since Boo Ferriss threw a six-hit shutout.

15 Selections for the honor of MVP are almost always debatable, but these are the three Red Sox players who were named Series MVPs the three times that (so far) the Sox have won the Series in the current century:
2004: Manny Ramirez
2007: Mike Lowell
2013: David Ortiz

Of the three, Ortiz would be the most difficult to question. He hit for a .688 batting average with two home runs (and four intentional walks) and six RBIs. Ramirez and Lowell's stats were almost identical—both had one home run and drove in four runs, Manny hit .412 and Mike hit .400.

16 The case would be for George Whiteman, in 1918. He's hardly a household name. But as we just saw, the Red Sox only scored nine runs in the entire 1918 World Series. Whiteman only batted .250—but that was the highest batting average of anyone on the team. The team's collective batting average was .186. Whiteman was involved—one way or another—in scoring five of Boston's nine runs. He also made dramatic catches in the outfield in Games One and Six. The one in Game Six was said by some to have saved the game for Boston.

17 For different reasons. The 1903 World Series was a best-of-nine competition between Pittsburg and Boston, and it took eight games before one team (the Boston Americans) reached the requisite five wins. In 1912, Game Two ended in a 6–6, 11-inning tie, before darkness arrived. The New York Giants had taken a 5–4 lead in the top of the eighth, but the Red Sox tied it up. Then the Giants scored in the top of the 10th to go ahead, 6–5, but again Boston tied it up.

18 Yes, there was—and it was in a Series that ran six games. First, consider one reason the Red Sox scored so few runs in 1915 yet won. They won Game Two by the score of

2–1, Game Three by the score of 2–1, and Game Four by the score of 2–1. They could have been marginally a little more efficient, but not much more.

Now, let's look at the 1918 World Series. It did run six games, not five, but the Red Sox only scored nine runs all Series long. Consider these scores:

Game One: Red Sox 1, Cubs 0
Game Two: Cubs 3, Red Sox 1
Game Three: Red Sox 2, Cubs 1
Game Four: Red Sox 3, Cubs 2
Game Five: Cubs 3, Red Sox 0
Game Six: Red Sox 2, Cubs 1

Nine runs in six games, and a world championship.

19 He was Tom Hughes, who was 20–7 with a 2.75 ERA in the 1903 regular season. He started Game Three of the World Series against the Pittsburg Pirates, but after giving up three runs (two earned) in two-plus innings, manager Jimmy Collins removed him and asked Cy Young to take over. Just a couple of months later, Hughes was traded to New York. Cy Young's biographer Reed Browning asked the question in print: "Could the gamblers have gotten to Hughes, and might Collins have suspected as much?"

As it worked out, Collins saw Hughes lose 23 games in 1904 and 20 games in 1905.

By the way, readers who would like to learn more about the Red Sox in the World Series are encouraged to read the book *From the Babe to the Beards,* by Bill Nowlin and Jim Prime, published by Sports Publishing in 2014.

20 It was none other than the Flyin' Hawaiian, Shane Victorino. Up to that point, he'd had just two hits (one single and one double) in 23 at-bats. His ALCS batting average was .125. You think he cared much?

And in the final game of the 2013 World Series against the St. Louis Cardinals, riding an 0-for-10 streak over the first three games, Victorino came up with the bases loaded again in the bottom of the third. This time, he doubled and drove in three. Later in the game, he drove in the sixth run of the game, too (Boston won, 6–1, and four of the RBIs were Victorino's). So he was .154 in the World Series.

21 Outfielder Harry Hooper played for the 1912, 1915, 1916, and 1918 world championship Red Sox teams. David Ortiz played for three (2004, 2007, and 2013). In the three World Series in which David Ortiz has played, his career batting average is .455.

Big Papi slugs another one.

Heinie Wagner was actually on the same four teams as Hooper, but he only appeared in six games in 1916 and three games in 1918.

8

FENWAY PARK

Let's kick off with a few attendance questions. Lots of people know about the incredible streak of 820 consecutive sold-out games at Fenway Park (794 regular-season games and 26 playoff games), which began on May 15, 2003 and ran into 2013.

1 What was the smallest crowd ever for a Red Sox game at Fenway Park? *(Answer on page 131.)*

2 What was the smallest crowd Fenway Park has ever drawn for an entire homestand? *(Answer on page 131.)*

3 What is considered to be the largest crowd to attend a Red Sox game at Fenway Park? *(Answer on page 132.)*

4 Which one person drew a larger crowd to Fenway Park than almost any Red Sox team ever has? *(Answer on page 133.)*

5 Is it true that the Red Sox team once almost got arrested for attempting to play a baseball game at Fenway Park? *(Answer on page 133.)*

6 It's well known that the Red Sox once gave a tryout to Jackie Robinson at Fenway Park in April 1945. Robinson reportedly was given high marks by Hugh Duffy, who ran the tryout, but he never heard from the Red Sox again, and it was fourteen years before the Red Sox fielded an African American ballplayer of their own: Pumpsie Green. This, despite Robinson becoming Rookie of the Year in the National League in 1947. The Red Sox thus failed to earn the distinction of being the first team to field a black ballplayer. Instead, as it transpired, they were the last. What else did the Red Sox fail to do on that day in April? *(Answer on page 135.)*

7 Who was the first African American baseball player to play in a regular-season game at Fenway Park? *(Answer on page 135.)*

8 What surprise awaited Pumpsie Green when he went to spring training for the first time with the Boston Red Sox, in 1959? *(Answer on page 137.)*

9 Cy Young won 511 games in his career, 192 of them for Boston. With the ballclub, his career ERA was precisely 2.00. Did he pitch better at home, or was he a road warrior? How many of his 192 wins were at Fenway Park? *(Answer on page 137.)*

10 Another tricky question? Can you name the only batter—for either team—who drove in more than 100 runs in a single season at Fenway Park? *(Answer on page 138.)*

11 Which of the following sports has never been featured at a Fenway Park event? *(Answer on page 138.)*

A. Football

B. Basketball

C. Soccer

D. Wrestling

E. Boxing

F. Lacrosse

G. Hurling

H. Snowboarding

I. Freeskiing

12 What date was the earliest in the calendar year when a regular-season game was played in Fenway Park? *(Answer on page 139.)*

A. January 1

B. March 20

C. March 30

D. April 1

13 When was it that the Red Sox were the visiting team during a regular-season game at Fenway Park? *(Answer on page 139.)*

FENWAY PARK
ANSWERS

1 July 14, 1922, or October 1, 1964? Though books on
the Red Sox typically cite 409 as the lowest paid attendance at a home Red Sox game (September 29, 1965), the
July 15, 1922, *Chicago Tribune* reported that only 68 fans
attended Fenway Park on July 14: "Exactly sixty-eight
people, and the figures are not exaggerated, sat in the
grand stand this afternoon . . . the turnout was the smallest of the season. This small attendance was approached
other days during the year." We have to question the
count, in that not one of five daily papers in Boston indi-
cates any fewer than 2,800 in attendance.

These look to be the lowest two totals that are verified by
more than one newspaper:

October 1, 1964 (Cleveland Indians at Boston): 306
fans. Boston 4, California 2

September 28, 1917 (St. Louis Browns at Boston): 356
fans. St. Louis 2, Boston 1

2 Consider these two games:

September 28, 1965 (California Angels at Boston): 461
fans. California 4, Boston 3

September 29, 1965 (California Angels at Boston: 409
fans. Boston 2, California 1

The two games played on September 28 and 29, 1965, represented the full homestand against the visiting Angels. Total attendance for the homestand came to 870.

3 Wes Ferrell was going for his 25th win of the season, and the Yankees were in town. On September 22, 1935, the official attendance was reported as 47,627. It was a doubleheader, and patrons were crammed into the park with as many as 5,000 standing on the field itself behind ropes in right field and right-center field. The Yankees hit seven ground-rule doubles into the crowd, and the Sox lost both games. That figure topped the 46,766 paid attendance on August 12, 1934—though there were said to be 48,000 in attendance at the 1934 game. In addition to the fans who somehow managed to get in, *The New York Times* said that "outside the portals of the park some 15,000 more stormed and fumed because they could get no nearer to the scene."

The largest crowd the Red Sox played before in the regular season was 83,533 (paid attendance of 81,841). *The New York Times* reports that an additional 511 paid to get in but had their money refunded to them because they simply couldn't find a vantage point from which watch the game. On top of that, the paper said that another "five or six thousand fought a hopeless battle to get in after the ticket booths were ordered closed." The date was May 30, 1938. It was a doubleheader at Yankee Stadium. The Red Sox lost both games, 10–0 and 5–4.

We've seen another question and answer mention the 115,300 paid attendance to the March 30, 2008, exhibition game in Los Angeles.

4 President Franklin D. Roosevelt, on November 4, 1944, closing his campaign for an unprecedented (and now impossible) fourth term as President of the United States. He drew a turnout reported as "over 40,000" (*Boston Globe*) in what proved to be the last campaign speech of his career. There were another 3,000 said to be outside on Lansdowne Street.

FDR's appearance was more or less equaled by that of Democratic candidate for the Presidency, Senator Eugene McCarthy, on July 25, 1968. The *Globe*'s front page headlined "45,000 Overflow Fenway Park for McCarthy," though it counted "close to 40,000" inside and said that "thousands more (at least 5,000)—many with tickets—were left standing in the street unable to get in. A dozen hung from the billboard in left field."

5 From *Red Sox Threads*: The time the Red Sox almost got arrested for playing a game at Fenway Park—a time in 1918 that the Red Sox almost got arrested for trying to raise money for the Red Cross. What? Harry Hooper, Babe Ruth, and company hauled off in handcuffs for violating the Sabbath law in Boston?

Playing baseball on Sundays had long been prohibited in Boston, but a delegation from the American Red Cross visited Fenway Park on May 24, 1918, and came to agreement with owner Harry Frazee that a regular scheduled game would be played on Sunday the 26th against the White Sox. Chicago owner Charles Comiskey was happy to agree to move the Monday game ahead to Sunday instead. The entire proceeds of the game were to go to the Red Cross. Regular ticket prices would apply, but box seats would be auctioned off to the public to raise even more money for the cause. Frazee agreed that the Red Sox would absorb the cost of staging the game. League President Ban Johnson readily agreed, as well.

With the World War on in earnest, the Red Cross could use all the money it could raise. It was estimated that between $40,000 and $50,000 would be raised—a major sum by the standards of the day.

The state legislature had passed legislation permitting Army and Navy service teams to play on Sundays, provided no admission was charged, and it was reported that both state and city authorities had given permission for the game.

Massachusetts Governor Samuel W. McCall supported the effort. So did Boston Mayor Andrew J. Peters, who signed a license to permit the game. The Attorney General of the Commonwealth ruled that the mayor had the authority to approve the license. The game was widely advertised in Boston newspapers. Everything looked great—it was motherhood and apple pie and a patriotic fundraiser for a needy cause.

Late on Saturday afternoon, Boston Police Commissioner Stephen O'Meara stepped in with a communiqué to Superintendent of Police Michael H. Crowley, declaring the proposed game in violation of the law, in that admission would be charged, and instructing Crowley that "police procedure should be to secure the names of persons taking part in or promoting it and apply to the court for summonses for them." It was actually a fine line the commissioner was taking; his lengthy statement in effect passed the buck on to the courts. The two police officials anticipated the possibility that the court would decline to issue summonses "or, having granted them, acquit the defendants." In that case, however, the superintendent warned, "the police will assume that such games are lawful and will thereafter treat them as games played on weekdays."

No one wanted to see the police taking names and prosecuting the case, so the game was scrapped and the Monday schedule adhered to, with ballclubs agreeing to donate the full proceeds of that game instead.

When the game was held on Monday, only $5,500 was raised, and a good half of that was said to have been the result of money bid for Sunday seats in the auction that the winning bidders let ride. Well under $3,000 was raised by virtue of tickets sold for the game itself. To make matters worse, Boston lost, 6–4.

6 They failed to sign Sam Jethroe. Aside from Robinson, two other ballplayers tried out that day—Marvin Williams and Sam Jethroe. Jethroe later signed with the Boston Braves and was voted Rookie of the Year in 1950. In one tryout, then, the Red Sox failed to sign two ballplayers, both of whom went on to become a rookie of the year (Robinson in 1947 and Jethroe in 1950).

7 The first time a black major-league player competed at Fenway Park was July 25, 1947. The player was a St. Louis Browns outfielder long ignored by history: right fielder Willard "Home Run" Brown. The very next day, the Browns featured two African American ballplayers in the same game, as second baseman Hank Thompson

joined Brown. See Chris Wertz's article on this Fenway first in the book *Pumpsie and Progress*. The same book also contains information on four Negro League games that were played at Fenway Park in 1942 and 1943. Was the Fenway Park crowd inhospitable to the Browns ballplayers? Hardly. As Wertz writes: "The nearly sold-out Fenway Park, 34,059 strong, gave him, a visiting player, applause. He responded by hitting a line-drive double off the center-field fence, later scoring on a single by first baseman Judnich. When he trotted out to right field at the end of the inning, they applauded again. And again, when he batted for the second time, they applauded. Brown responded with his second double of the night—the second of his career. With each plate appearance and each time he took his position in right field, the Fenway faithful greeted Willard Brown with cheers which grew as the game progressed. According to Jack Barry of the *Boston Evening Globe*, '[Brown] received a fine ovation from the crowd as he trotted to his right field position at the close of each round.' The next day the *St. Louis Post-Dispatch* reported, 'Willard Brown, the cat-walking Negro right-fielder of the Browns, who runs like a hurried panther, last night earned some of the loudest cheering Boston has given to a visiting ball player here in years.'"

Was this an anomaly? Not really, it appears. Boston Braves fans welcomed Sam Jethroe when he joined the Braves in 1950—the same Sam Jethroe who'd tried out for the Red Sox in April 1945 at Fenway Park. See the article by Bill Nowlin, "How Sam Jethroe Was Received in Boston" at: thenationalpastimemuseum.com/article/how-sam-jethroe-was-received-boston.

8 He was not allowed to stay at the team hotel because of the color of his skin. It was the Safari Hotel in Scottsdale, Arizona, and African Americans were not allowed to stay in Scottsdale overnight. "Arrangements have been made for Green to stay in a plush hotel in Phoenix," explained traveling secretary Tom Dowd. In fact, he stayed at the hotel where the Giants stayed. The notion that the Red Sox might have themselves switched hotels seems not to have been suggested.

9 Trick question, sorry. He never won a game at Fenway Park. He couldn't have. Cy Young's last year in the

Cy Young of the Boston Americans.

majors was 1911, split between Cleveland and the Boston Braves, and Fenway Park didn't open until 1912.

10 Deceptive phrasing? "Either club?" Of course, it could really only be a Red Sox player. No other team plays enough games at Fenway Park to make it even remotely likely that a visiting player could drive in 100 runs in one season at any one ballpark. Even for a Red Sox player, it's hard to imagine someone could drive in 100 runs in a park where they only play half their games. But Jimmie Foxx did it in 1938. He drove in 104 runs at Fenway Park that year. He still holds the Red Sox record for most RBIs in a season (175); he drove in 71 on the road and 104 at home in Fenway.

11 Actually, every one of them has been featured at Fenway at one time or another over the years. Fenway Park had also hosted more than 360 high school football games, 45 college football games, and an even 100 professional football games from the Boston Shamrocks, the Boston Redskins, the Boston Bears, the Boston Yanks, and, in the 1960s, the Boston Patriots before they became the New England Patriots. The Pats played their first home game at Braves Field but from 1963 through 1968 called Fenway Park home. In more recent years, the Patriots won three Super Bowls in the first years of the twenty-first century, sharing back-to-back wins in the year the Red Sox won the 2004 World Series.

There have also been two Gaelic football matches played at Fenway and 26 soccer matches (the game the rest of the world calls football).

Fenway Park has also hosted 22 professional boxing bouts, 17 pro wrestling events, six lacrosse games, three ice hockey matches, two basketball games, and even a hurling match—and not the kind of hurling that you occasionally see in the bleachers. The final three sports listed—hurling and the two snow events—were all staged during the 2015–16 offseason. There had been hurling once before, though, in 1916 and again in 1954.

12 OK, this one was a trick question, as well. It was A: January 1.

On January 1, 2010, the Boston Bruins played a regular-season National Hockey League game at Fenway Park, beating the Philadelphia Flyers in overtime, 2–1. They had pulled even from a 1–0 deficit with only 1:57 remaining in the third period to force overtime. It was a game in which the higher-priced field box seats were the worst seats in the house, since patrons there couldn't see the puck due to the wall around the rink. The game was, quite naturally, another sold-out Fenway affair.

13 July 24, 1994. What's the story? Five days earlier, on July 19, the Seattle Mariners were at home taking batting practice. Just a half an hour before the gates opened to the public, four ceiling tiles from the roof of the Kingdome fell onto the seats. Each tile weighed approximately 26 pounds. Fortunately, no one was hurt. The game was canceled, and the Mariners played the rest of their "home games" on the road. The first four home games they played out of town were 3,000 miles away, at Boston's

Fenway Park. The first was on July 22. Naturally, no seats had been sold, so the Red Sox put the last-minute tickets on sale at old-fashioned prices: $10 for a grandstand seat. Home-field advantage may not have counted for much; Boston lost the first game, 6–3, with Seattle's Randy Johnson outpitching Aaron Sele. There was a single-admission doubleheader played the next day, a split. Boston won the July 24 game. Although these were purportedly home games for Seattle, Boston batted last and consequently never batted in the bottom of the ninth in the two games they won.

Ever hopeful of adding another Red Sox autograph.

9

PERSONALITIES

1 Is it true that a member of the Red Sox was once given a pistol and sent on an assassination mission to prevent Nazi Germany from developing the atomic bomb? *(Answer on page 147.)*

2 For twenty-six years, Sherm Feller served the Red Sox as public address announcer. For a few years, before MLB took over team websites, opening the Red Sox site treated computer users with the audio recording of Feller saying, "Ladies and gentlemen, boys and girls, welcome to Fenway Park." What other notable talent did Feller have? *(Answer on page 148.)*

3 Who leads the Red Sox in ejections from ballgames? *(Answer on page 148.)*
   A. Wes Ferrell
   B. Terry Francona
   C. Ted Williams
   D. Carl Yastrzemski

E. Babe Ruth

F. Jimmy Piersall

4 On January 9, 1910, the *Boston Globe* reported that this ballplayer asked Red Sox manager Patsy Donovan in 1910 "if his color would prevent him getting a trial in Boston, and was assured that Boston was looking for speed boys willing to hustle." The Red Sox signed him, and he played for the team that year. Who was he? *(Answer on page 148.)*

5 Which Red Sox manager said he didn't believe in pitchers having their arms looked after by professional trainers? *(Answer on page 150.)*

6 Chick Stahl was the first (and only) Red Sox manager to commit suicide—during spring training in 1907. "Boys, you drove me to it," he wrote in a somewhat ambiguous suicide note. Who was the only Red Sox manager to be convicted of homicide? *(Answer on page 150.)*

7 Which Red Sox manager who ran the team for at least 200 games had the best managerial winning percentage? *(Answer on page 150.)*

A. Joe Cronin

B. Terry Francona

C. Bill Carrigan

D. Don Zimmer

E. Joe Morgan

F. Dick Williams

8 Is it true that at one point, John W. Henry owned parts of both the Red Sox and the New York Yankees? *(Answer on page 150.)*

9 Red Sox manager Dick Williams once famously said, "There'll be no captains on this team" and in the process let Carl Yastrzemski ("Captain Carl") know that he was to be considered a member of the team, not a player with special status. Since Yaz, only two Red Sox players have been named team captain. Can you name them? *(Answer on page 151.)*

10 When he took charge himself, what change in the clubhouse did incoming manager Bobby Valentine proclaim in February 2012? *(Answer on page 151.)*

11 An earlier manager, Joe McCarthy, came to the Red Sox from the Yankees, who have always maintained fairly strict policies regarding player dress and grooming. Responding to questions as to what he was going to do in managing Ted Williams, who was widely known for his distaste for neckties, what did McCarthy do? *(Answer on page 151.)*

12 Was it true that the Red Sox signing of David Ortiz was described at the time as an example of "shopping at Wal-Mart"? *(Answer on page 151.)*

13 It wasn't that long ago. At one point in 2005, in entirely separate events, two different Red Sox relief pitchers were both reported as having been victims of kidnapping. Can you name the two? *(Answer on page 152.)*

14 Did Ted Williams once play professional football? And did he once play for the Yanks? *(Answer on page 153.)*

15 And, speaking of football, true or false: Dom DiMaggio once was an owner of the Patriots? *(Answer on page 153.)*

16 And, speaking of Dom DiMaggio, Ted Williams was "The Kid," Johnny Pesky was "Needlenose," and Bobby Doerr was "The Silent Captain." What was Dominic? *(Answer on page 153.)*

17 What Hall of Fame ballplayer, born as Aloys Szymanski, once played for the Red Sox? *(Answer on page 153.)*

18 The Red Sox were, notably, the last team in the majors to integrate, in 1959 when Pumpsie Green signed with the Sox. In 1962, in a move to seek out more "Negro talent," the Red Sox actually hired a former "clown" to serve as their scout. True or false? *(Answer on page 153.)*

19 Kind of an easy one. What Red Sox player was signed out of St. Mary's Industrial School for Orphans, Delinquent, Incorrigible, and Wayward Boys? *(Answer on page 154.)*

20 What former Red Sox player later became a candidate for president of the United States on the Rhinoceros Party ticket? *(Answer on page 154.)*

21 OK, so Ted Williams and several of Boston's sportswriters didn't exactly get along. But on "Ted Williams Day"—April 30, 1952, the last day Williams played for the Red Sox before rejoining the U.S. Marine Corps at the time of the Korean War—what did nemesis Dave Egan suggest? *(Answer on page 155.)*

22 Who holds the record for stolen bases in a single season for the Red Sox? *(Answer on page 255.)*

23 Can you match the Red Sox personnel with the animals in question? *(Answer on page 156.)*

A. Don Zimmer	1. Pigeon
B. Ed Jurak	2. Bird
C. Ellis Kinder	3. Gerbil
D. Ted Williams	4. Cat
E. Felix Mantilla	5. Dog
F. Mo Vaughn	6. Rat

24 Can you name at least 10 Red Sox players who have the same names as presidents of the United States? Two modest exclusions: there has never been an Obama who played for the Red Sox, nor a Garciaparra who was president. *(Answer on page 156.)*

PERSONALITIES ANSWERS

1 Basically. A former member, anyhow. He wasn't meant to actually do it in full uniform. (For what it's worth, which is almost nothing, Berg wore #19 in his season with the Sox, and then #22 thereafter.) Backup catcher Moe Berg played for the Red Sox from 1935 through 1939, his last years in the major leagues. In January 1942, within weeks after Pearl Harbor, he volunteered to join the OSS, the predecessor to today's CIA. He was assigned to Europe and based in Rome. He spoke German well and prepped enough in physics to be able to converse on the subject at a conference in Zurich that Germany's Werner Heisenberg was attending. His goal was to determine whether the Nazis were working to develop atomic weaponry and, if so, how far along they might be.

As the CIA's Linda McCarthy wrote in the book *When Baseball Went to War*, "Moe was armed with pistol (to eradicate Heisenberg if he uttered anything alluding to a *Wunderwaffe*) and a lethal cyanide or 'L' pill (for the secret operative, if he were captured and tortured). Scribbling pages of notes, Moe leaned on Heisenberg's lecture. Observing the crowd's reaction to it, as well as

Heisenberg's delivery and demeanor, Moe gleaned nothing from the evening's events that hinted Hitler had embarked on a campaign to build an atomic bomb.

"Later, at an informal get-together Moe attended, Heisenberg openly despaired of Germany's ongoing reversal of fortunes. To OSS operative Moe Berg, Heisenberg's revealing comments meant Germany had no weapon on the scale of America's Little Boy and Fat Man in production. The baseball-player-turned-spy had, as they say in the intel biz, proved a negative."

2 He wrote music. His most widely-known composition was the rock song "Summertime, Summertime" and the standard "Snow, Snow, Beautiful Snow." But Feller also wrote a symphony that was performed by the Boston Pops, "John Kennedy Symphony."

3 It's Terry Francona. Among ballplayers, Yaz (with 11) leads the pack. Second and third are Sammy White (9) and Jimmy Piersall (8). Difficult as this may be to believe, given all the publicity given to a reputation built up about him, Ted Williams was never once ejected from a ballgame.

4 He was Native American Louis LeRoy. He was a "Stockbridge-Munsee" Indian, a group of Mohicans, and was taught in reservation schools growing up and then attended the famous Carlisle Indian Industrial School in Pennsylvania. Jimmy Collins had tried to sign LeRoy years earlier but was told that he was not free to accept outside work until graduation because "the US

Jimmy Piersall and a couple of happy admirers.

government had a claim on the Indian." When he finally was signed, by Donovan, the *Boston Globe* reported that the contract of "Leroy, the Indian" was in hand. For the full SABR biography of LeRoy, see Bill Nowlin's bio of him at: sabr.org/bioproj/person/b0cb6bb0.

5 Same guy. Patsy Donovan. He amplified: "Cy Young was one of the great pitchers who had no use for the rubbing and kneading that many pitchers are subject to, on the advice of the trainers." *Boston Globe*, January 28, 1910.

6 On January 15, 1969, Mike "Pinky" Higgins was sentenced to four years of hard labor in the Louisiana State Prison after pleading guilty to negligent homicide when his car went out of control and killed a highway worker. He had been fired by the Red Sox on September 16, 1965. In February 1968, he was reportedly intoxicated and hit three workers with his car. Because of a bad heart, he was paroled after serving only two months in prison. Some 48 hours after his release, he was dead of a heart attack.

7 The top winning percentages for Red Sox managers with 200 or more games are:
Don Zimmer: .575 (411–304)
Terry Francona: .574 (744–502)
Jimmy Collins: .548 (455–376)
Joe Cronin: .539 (1071–916)
Dick Williams: .545 (260–217)
Jimy Williams: .540 (414–352)

8 It is true. And he owned the Marlins, too. On January 16, 2002, Major League Baseball voted 29–0 (the Yankees abstained) to approve the sale of the Red Sox from the Yawkey trust (the JRY Trust) to a group headed by John W. Henry, Tom Werner, and Larry Lucchino. Henry owned the Marlins at the time and was given approval to sell that team, which he did before the end of February. As it happens, Henry also owned a 1 percent stake in the New York Yankees, which he disposed of on February 27, the day the sale of the Red Sox occurred. It's likely the transactions were timed so that while Henry owned part of the Yankees on February 27 and part of the Red Sox on February 27, the sale of the Yankees interest occurred minutes before the purchase of the Red Sox.

9 Jim Rice and Jason Varitek. Yaz himself was renamed captain on March 22, 1974.

10 He announced that there would be no alcohol (not even beer) in the Red Sox clubhouse. David Ortiz said, "We're not here to drink. We're here to play baseball. It ain't a bar." Valentine's policy was seen as a reaction to the team falling apart in the last weeks of the prior season (2011), with accusations that some players were sending out to a nearby Popeye's for fried chicken and drinking beer in the clubhouse during games.

11 On February 29, 1948, he showed up in Sarasota, wearing a sports shirt and no necktie. "If I can't get along with a .400 hitter," he says, "I wouldn't be a very good manager."

12 That was only the most memorable phrase among what seemed like a unanimously underwhelming reaction from the Boston press. Gordon Edes of the *Boston Globe* wrote of the signing, "the Red Sox all but completed a winter of shopping at Wal-Mart, yesterday announcing the signing of free agent first baseman David Ortiz." (*Globe*, January 23, 2003, a story that was well balanced and holds up well enough when read more than a dozen years later.) Here's a challenge: try to find another Boston writer who felt otherwise. The Boston press was far from impressed when the January 22, 2003, signing was announced, as Alan Siegel of *Boston* magazine noted in a March 12, 2013, daily article.

All credit to Theo Epstein of the Red Sox for seeing the talent in Twins first baseman David Ortiz. Ortiz had hit an unheralded 20 homers in 2002, though even Epstein seemed to consider the signing as a way to supplement the signing of first baseman Jeremy Giambi. Apparently, there are exceptional bargains to be had at Walmart.

13 The first one was the only Red Sox player with the initials U. U. U.—Ugueth Urbina. His mother, Maura Villareal, had been kidnapped since September 1, 2004, and had been held more than four months for a ransom of a few million dollars. Rich "El Guapo" Garces was reported missing, and it was feared that he, too, had been kidnapped in his native Venezuela. Garces had often expressed his fears of being held for ransom. On January 30, it was reported that Garces was in fact in fine shape. He'd been away for 10 days—at a beach party. Sra. Villareal was shortly rescued in what Mark Townsend of Big League Stew described as a "successful commando-style rescue operation." Two of the kidnappers were killed in a gun battle with police. Urbina himself was arrested later in the year and convicted of the (apparently unrelated) attempted murder of three farm workers in an incident involving a machete and gasoline.

14 Yes, to both. Born in Bulls Bay, Canada, in 1916, Theodore Patrick "Ted" Williams played football for both Boston College and Notre Dame (remarkable in its own right) and was selected in the third round of the 1942 NFL draft by the Philadelphia Eagles. He played in 11 games for the Eagles in 1942. In 1944, he played 10 games as halfback for the Boston Yanks. Fenway Park was the Yanks' home field.

15 It's true. He was a cofounder of the team and, along with Billy Sullivan and Paul Sonnabend, one of ten owners of the Boston Patriots.

16 Dom DiMaggio was known as "The Little Professor."

17 Al Simmons. In his 20-year major-league career, the only year he played for the Red Sox was during World War II—1943. The former two-time American League batting champion hit .203 in 141 at-bats, even against the depleted pitching during wartime ball.

18 This is true. In 1962, Ed Scott was hired as the team's first full-time scout to seek out African American ballplayers for Boston. Scott was a former outfielder with the Indianapolis Clowns of the old Negro Leagues. Among the players he signed for the Red Sox were George Scott (unrelated) and Oil Can Boyd. He is also the scout who first signed Hank Aaron, but that had been ten years before he was hired by the Red Sox. Once on board, Ed Scott worked for the Red Sox for forty years.

19 George H. Ruth, signed by Jack Dunn of the Baltimore Orioles in 1914. Less than five months later, Babe Ruth was playing for the Boston Red Sox.

20 With a moment's reflection, could it have been anyone other than Bill Lee? This happened in 1988. He was

Bill Lee with his Ho Chi Minh goatee, at the time he wrote *The Little Red (Sox) Book* with Jim Prime.

running against Gov. Michael Dukakis (D) of Massachusetts and George H. W. Bush (R), who won. Lee had said he'd be glad to accept the VP slot for either of the two major parties, provided it didn't interfere with playing baseball. Both Dukakis and Bush looked elsewhere for their running mates.

21 Egan suggested that rather than honor Williams, civic leaders should "officially horsewhip" him because of the "vicious influence that he had had on the childhood of America."

In what might well have proved to be his last at-bat in major-league baseball, Williams hit a two-run homer off Dizzy Trout his very last time up, to break a 3–3 tie with the Tigers and win the game for the Red Sox, 5–3.

22 Jacoby Ellsbury. He stole 70 bases in 2009, obliterating the mark of 54 previously held by Tommy Harper

Jacoby Ellsbury signing for fans.

(1973). Remarkably, the first 25 times in his career that Ellsbury attempted to steal a base, he succeeded. His first "caught stealing" only came on his 26th attempt. Some years later, on May 30, 2013, Ellsbury stole five bases in one game. That's not something you can do unless you get on base to begin with.

23 Here are the matches:

Don Zimmer was famously dubbed a gerbil by Bill Lee.

Ed Jurak once trapped a rat during a game on the field at Fenway.

Ellis Kinder once hit a low-swooping bird while pitching at Fenway Park.

Ted Williams, on more than one occasion, used a shotgun to help rid the park of pigeons.

Mantilla was known as "Felix the Cat."

Mo Vaughn was the "Hit Dog."

Other players we could have included are Mike "Gator" Greenwell, "the Hawk" Ken Harrelson, Birdie Tebbetts, and many, many more.

24 Here's the list. How many did you get?

Bob ADAMS/Terry ADAMS

Ike BOONE/Ray BOONE

Bullet Joe BUSH

Chris CARTER

Reggie CLEVELAND

TRUMAN Clevenger

Lu CLINTON

THOMAS JEFFERSON Dowd

Frankie HAYES

Conor JACKSON/Damian JACKSON/Ron JACKSON

Reggie JEFFERSON

Bob JOHNSON (and Brian, Deron, Earl, Hank, Jason,
    John Henry, Kelly, Rankin, Roy, & Vic JOHNSON)

Bill KENNEDY/John KENNEDY

Trot NIXON/Russ NIXON/Willard NIXON/Otis
    NIXON

Jeff PIERCE

Harry TAYLOR/Scott TAYLOR

Jermaine VAN BUREN

BENJAMIN HARRISON Van Dyke

Alex WILSON (and Archie, Duane, Earl, Gary, Jack,
    Jim, John, Lee, Hal, and Squanto WILSON)

Stretching a little, we could consider Bill REGAN.

10

ODD ITEMS

1 How did the team ever come to be named the Red Sox in the first place? Because they wore red socks? Yes, but the story is a lot odder than that. What's the story? *(Answer on page 165.)*

2 No love lost? Babe Ruth was sold to the Yankees in December 1919. The last home game of the 1919 Red Sox season had been declared "Babe Ruth Day," and Ruth responded by hitting his league-leading 27th homer of the season, tying the 1884 record held by Ned Williamson. He won the game for Boston. What special treat did Red Sox owner Harry Frazee have for Ruth? *(Answer on page 166.)*

3 Which owner of the Red Sox (if any) was born in Boston? Was there ever an owner who was foreign-born? OK, it's two questions in one. *(Answer on page 166.)*

4 The Red Sox have had a lot of uniquely named players over the years. There's never been another major leaguer with the name "Nomar" and never one named "Garciaparra." There have been surnames from Agbayani and Badenhop to Zauchin and Zupcic. Has there ever been a Red Sox player with as bland a name as "John Smith"? *(Answer on page 166.)*

5 A picture of the Red Sox sold for more than $20 million in 2014. Was it Dave Roberts and "The Steal" in 2004? If not, which picture was it? *(Answer on page 167.)*

6 Which Red Sox player of recent years was struck and killed by lightning? *(Answer on page 167.)*

7 Can you remember whom the Red Sox traded to get Bill Buckner? They traded two players. One was Mike Brumley. Who was the other one? *(Answer on page 167.)*

8 Which Red Sox player once hit a home run off his own brother and then later both he and his brother were traded away in the same deal? *(Answer on page 167.)*

9 The perfect comeback? On July 6, 2012, Red Sox fans who were in their seats at the start of the game saw the Yankees score five runs in the top of the first inning. Fans who had only just arrived at that very point might have been tempted to just turn around and walk back out of Fenway Park. What happened next? *(Answer on page 168.)*

10 How did Billy Werber's patience, daring, and speed win an extra-inning game for the Red Sox? *(Answer on page 168.)*

11 Four members of the Red Sox were chosen the MVP of an All-Star Game. Three of them are Carl Yastrzemski in 1970, Roger Clemens in 1986, and Pedro Martinez in 1999 (at Fenway Park, no less). Who is the fourth? *(Answer on page 168.)*

12 In 1972, Carlton Fisk hit 22 homers and batted .293. He was named Rookie of the Year and was awarded a Gold Glove. He was named to the All-Star team for the first of 11 times. How many other times during his major-league career was Fisk named Rookie of the Year? *(Answer on page 169.)*

13 One of the odder questions: was there a time when a moose that had somehow gotten ahold of a motor vehicle managed to hit a Red Sox player on the field in the middle of a ballgame? *(Answer on page 169.)*

14 Far from being odd, this just seemed like a nicer note to end on: What is the official charity of the Boston Red Sox? *(Answer on page 169.)*

Last Question: Can you name the author who has written or edited more books about the Red Sox than anyone else in major-league history?

A. Bill Nowlin has written or edited, prior to this one, more than 40 books on the Boston Red Sox, including *Red Sox Threads* and *Day by Day with the Boston Red Sox,* Johnny Pesky's biography, and several books about Ted Williams. He's also edited a number of "team books" on the Red Sox, in collaboration with colleagues from the Society of American Baseball Research (SABR), which he serves as vice president. Among the SABR books are *The 1967 Impossible Dream Red Sox* and books on the 1901 Boston Americans, the 1912 Red Sox and the opening of Fenway Park, the 1918 Sox, the 1939 team, the 1948 team, the Red Sox of the 1950s, the 1975 team, and the 1986 Red Sox. With Allan Wood, he wrote *Don't Let Us Win Tonight! An Oral History of the 2004 Boston Red Sox's Impossible Playoff Run.* He's also worked on a couple of dozen other books, usually for SABR, on subjects such as scouts, umpires, subjects inspired by The Simpsons (see the book coedited with Emily Hawks, *Nuclear-Powered Baseball*), etc.

A lifelong fan born in Boston, Bill has seen Ted Williams hit, enjoyed four no-hitters at Fenway Park, taken in Roger Clemens's first 20-strikeout game, thrilled to Carlton Fisk's Game Six home run, and ranks as the most exciting game ever the Game Five walk off in the 2004 ALCS (though, admittedly, had the Sox not won the games that followed, that might now have seemed anticlimactic). He's stayed overnight—all night—at Fenway, as the night cleaning crew picked up after a game, and worked a couple of games inside the left-field scoreboard. He's lived some of the history he writes about in this volume, and even has a lifetime .333 batting average at Fenway Park—even if it was in a charity game.

After hundreds upon hundreds of games, there's still some of that excitement in going to any given game than there was at age 12. You never know what new thing you might see.

In 1970, Bill Nowlin was one of three friends who founded America's most active independent music label,

Rounder Records, which has produced over 3,000 albums of roots music. Dr. Nowlin also a former professor of political science who has continued to teach the occasional course as recently as spring 2016 ("Politics and Baseball") at what is now the University of Massachusetts at Lowell. He lives in Cambridge, Massachusetts, with his son Emmet, and in 2015 proved he can walk home from Fenway Park.

ODD ITEMS ANSWERS

1 It's something the author detailed at length in his 2008 book *Red Sox Threads*. On December 18, 1907, shortly after Boston's National League team revealed that the new uniforms for 1908 eliminated their customary red stockings, owner John I. Taylor of the Boston Americans pounced. He quickly decided that his team would adopt red hose and call themselves the Boston Red Sox. Taylor personally oversaw the uniform design, selecting red stockings because Boston's first professional baseball team—the Red Stockings—had worn them. Taylor appreciated the link with tradition. It was predicted that the name "Red Sox" would prove a popular choice.

Was Taylor imprudently putting the health, or even the lives of his players in jeopardy? Historian Ellery Clark wrote that the owners of the NL team, George and John Dovey, "decided the red dye in their club's stockings might well lead to blood infection and even worse if and when one or more of their players were cut in the leg by opposing spikes. The grand old color and the nickname were abandoned in the interests of health."

Rash though Taylor's decision may have been, generations of Red Sox players have come and gone with no documented case of red dye disease. It wasn't until the

2004 postseason that blood on the stockings played any noteworthy role in Red Sox lore.

The story of the original Boston Red Stockings (1871–75) is a fascinating one. For a look at that five-year stretch when Boston baseball dominated the competition (they started the 1875 season with a 26–0 record), see the book *Boston's First Nine: The 1871–1875 Boston Red Stockings* (SABR, 2016).

2 A cigar. Or, one could say, pretty much none at all. The following year, Ruth complained that Harry Frazee had made him "buy my wife's ticket to the game," adding, "Fifteen thousand fans show up and all I got was a cigar."

3 Joseph Lannin, owner from 1914–16, was born in Canada, and his first job was as a bellboy in a hotel. Clearly, he advanced in his career. No owner of the Red Sox was ever born in Boston, though John I. Taylor was born in neighboring Somerville, Massachusetts.

4 Yes, there has—and he's the only John Smith to ever play major-league baseball since 1882. John Marshall Smith was a switch-hitting first baseman for the Red Sox in 1931. He played four games in two days, back-to-back doubleheaders on September 17 and September 18. The Red Sox won three of the four games, but Smith was only 2-for-15 (.133). He drove in the only Red Sox run in a 2–1 loss in one of the games. That was his only career RBI. (In that same game, Earl Webb hit his 67th double of the season, setting the mark for most doubles in a single season, a mark that still stands today.) After baseball,

Mr. Smith went to Washington, and John Smith of the Red Sox took up work as a legal adviser for the IRS.

5   On May 22, 2014, "The Rookie"—Norman Rockwell's famous painting of the Red Sox locker room, depicting (among others) Ted Williams and Frank Sullivan—sold at a Christie's auction in New York for $22.6 million to an undisclosed bidder. It had first been a cover for the *Saturday Evening Post* in 1957.

6   On May 25, 2008, pitcher Geremi Gonzalez was struck by lightning and killed while water-skiing. Gonzalez was 2–1 for the Red Sox in 2005; he last pitched in the majors in 2006. The strike occurred in Venezuela. But that wasn't the strangest death of Red Sox alumni in Venezuela. On November 23, 1990, former Sox catcher Bo Diaz was crushed to death by a television satellite dish that fell on him while he was trying to adjust it on the roof of his home in Caracas. He was thirty-seven years old.

7   The other one was Dennis Eckersley. He pitched three years for the Cubs (1984, 1985, and 1986) before moving on to Oakland.

8   That would be Rick Ferrell. (He's in the Hall of Fame.) On July 19, 1933, Red Sox catcher Rick hit a three-run homer off Cleveland Indians pitcher Wes Ferrell, his brother. Wes was not pleased. The next year, in May 1934, the Red Sox acquired Wes in a trade, and the two brothers were both BoSox. On June 11, 1937, both Wes and Rick were traded

to Washington (along with outfielder Mel Almada, the first Mexican-born major leaguer). Wes won 193 big-league games. Rick held the Red Sox record for games caught as a catcher until Carlton Fisk broke it in 1988, four years after the Veterans Committee had voted Rick into the Hall of Fame. After baseball, Rick became a scout and advanced to become Detroit Tigers GM from 1959–74.

9 You probably guessed it. The Red Sox scored five runs in the bottom of the first inning, restoring the game to an even balance. Sox catcher Saltalamacchia (who still holds the record for most letters in a Red Sox player surname) hit a three-run homer. By the end of the game, however, the Red Sox lost, 10–8. On another odd note, this was the first game of a four-game series. The visiting Yankees scored five times in the top of the first inning of this first game, four times in the top of the first inning of the second game, three times in the top of the first in the third, and two times in the top of the first in the final game.

10 On July 7, 1935, Billy Werber drew a walk with one out in the bottom of the 13th inning in this game against the Philadelphia Athletics, the first game of a doubleheader. Werber then stole second, and, when Babe Dahlgren grounded out to second base, Werber sprinted all the way from second base to home and scored the winning run.

11 J. D. Drew in 2008. Maybe a bit of a surprise? It was the only year he was chosen to go to the All-Star Game, but he made the most of it. Ichiro Suzuki started the game in right field. After five innings (which probably seemed at the time it would be the midpoint of the game), Drew replaced him in the field. The game went on for 15 innings, the American League winning in the bottom of the 15th. Drew hit a two-run homer in the bottom of the seventh to tie the game, 2–2. The final run scored thanks to a sacrifice fly, probably not the sort of thing that earns an MVP. There were 23 pitchers in the game, so it would have been difficult to single out one for MVP honors. Drew's homer was the biggest offensive thing in the game, and it got him the nod.

12 You didn't fall for that one, did you? You can only be a rookie once.

13 Yes, there was. The moose was Mariner Moose, the mascot of the Seattle Mariners. The park was Safeco Field in Seattle. The date was August 5, 2007. The vehicle was an ATV. While taking the field in the middle of the fifth inning, Coco Crisp (Boston's center fielder) was struck by the vehicle but fortunately not seriously injured. It wasn't the only time a Sox player was struck by a piece of equipment at another ballpark. On September 19, 1989, Mike Greenwell was playing catch before the game when he was hit by a SkyDome maintenance tractor. He had to sit out that night's game.

14 It's actually changed a bit in recent years. For a half-century, it was the Jimmy Fund, the fundraising arm of the Dana-Farber Cancer Institute. The charity, founded to fight cancer in children, was initially the charity of the

Boston Braves, following a 1948 national radio broadcast of Ralph Edwards's *Truth or Consequences*, in which Edwards interviewed a young boy in a Boston hospital bed grievously ill with leukemia. The boy was given the name "Jimmy." His favorite team was the Braves, and during the broadcast several Braves paid a surprise visit to cheer him up. The pioneering work of Dr. Sidney Farber bought about considerable success. When he began, his idea of chemotherapy was mocked by many. Of course, today, it is a common treatment for many cancers. At the time, however, the diagnosis of leukemia was typically a virtual death sentence, and many patients were discharged to the comforts of their home, hospitals seeing no hope to care for them.

When the Braves left Boston to move to Milwaukee, owner Lou Perini paid a personal visit to Red Sox owner Tom Yawkey and asked him if the Red Sox would adopt the Jimmy Fund as their team charity. Yawkey agreed on the spot. Ted Williams had known Dr. Farber and appeared at least once in 1947—before the Braves became involved—and in later years became honorary chairman of the Jimmy Fund. Ironically, it was leukemia that claimed Tom Yawkey in the end, as well as Ted Williams's son John-Henry. The original Jimmy survived over fifty years from the 1948 broadcast and died of causes other than cancer.

For decades, a sign promoting the Jimmy Fund was the only sign allowed inside Fenway Park. There was to be no advertising. That changed, for economic reasons, under new ownership. When the new owners came in (the Henry/Werner/Lucchino group), they set up the

Red Sox Foundation. It is now the official charity of the Red Sox and has donated tens of millions of dollars to worthy causes. The Jimmy Fund is one of the featured charities to which the Red Sox Foundation donates.

There is another connection between the Red Sox and the Jimmy Fund. The last three chairmen of the Jimmy Fund have been Red Sox broadcaster Ken Coleman, former Red Sox second baseman Mike Andrews and, after a hiatus of several years, Larry Lucchino of the Red Sox—himself a two-time cancer survivor, treated at Dana-Farber both times.